RELISH
NORTH EAST

Original recipes from the region's finest chefs

First Published 2011
By Relish Publications
Shield Green Farm, Tritlington,
Northumberland NE61 3DX

ISBN 978-0-9564205-4-1

Publisher: Duncan L Peters
General Manager: Teresa Peters
Marketing and Design: Ria Parkin
Food Photography: NR & KG Photography
Landscape Photography: Graeme Peacock
Photographic Imagery
Proof Assistant: Jack Bamber
Printed By: Balto Print Ltd, Stratford,
London E15 2TF

RELISH
PUBLICATIONS.CO.UK

004
CONTENTS

DESSERTS

RESTAURANTS

006 CONTENTS

DESSERTS

INTRODUCTION WITH TERRY LAYBOURNE

Chef and restaurateur Terry Laybourne is something of an institution in his native North East England. Few people interested in good food and great hospitality have not heard of Terry or eaten in one of the restaurants within his 21 Hospitality Group. As the first chef to win and bring a Michelin star to Tyneside only four years after opening his own restaurant, 21 Queen Street, on Newcastle's Quayside in 1988, he was largely responsible for putting the area on the culinary map. Terry learned his craft in some of the finest hotels on continental Europe before returning to the North East to lead the kitchen of the newly opened Fisherman's Lodge in Jesmond Dene. But it was when he started his own restaurant that his career really took off. Critical acclaim and industry awards followed culminating in Terry being awarded the MBE for services to the restaurant industry and tourism. While growing his own group of restaurants he has worked as a consultant for hotels, Fenwick, Northumbrian Larder and Newcastle United. His enthusiasm shows no signs of slowing and he recently opened a new food-led pub in Newcastle, The Broad Chare, which is one of the restaurants featured in these pages.

I am delighted to be promoting this book, it is not simply a showcase for good cooking and great regional restaurants; it's also a celebration of the high quality of food and drink available in North East England.

Good cooking is about good shopping. Our best regional restaurants are only as good as their suppliers and the raw materials they provide.

What makes small, regionally-based producers successful is their determination to consider the quality of what they are making and to deliver it to the best of their ability, whatever the cost.

It's that ethos you see in all our restaurants and importantly, it's a philosophy that's been embraced by other restaurateurs within the last 10-20 years and is reflected among many of our best dining venues featured in this book. Today's best chefs recognise the value of working with artisan producers. By using the best produce and by adding some craft in the kitchen you can create a magical experience for those who enjoy great food.

The formula is quite simple. Good restaurants – whether they're country pubs, bistros, top hotels or fine dining establishments – provide good cooking when they're using good products, usually that are locally sourced, fresh, and seasonal. Here in the North East, we have real craftsmen working with nature to produce crops, seafood and meat bursting with flavour and freshness.

TV has turned some of our national chefs into rock-star celebrities, occasionally larger than life where the food has become an incidental. However, it's fair to say that many good chefs stick to what they love and are often uncomfortable venturing far from the kitchen. This is their studio and stage, where they apply their trade.

The chefs and restaurants in these pages make the food the stars, they include the Bouchon Bistrot in Hexham, Seaham Hall, Blackfriars in Newcastle, Battlesteads up near Hadrian's Wall, and Slaley Hall, along with our very own Masterchef Finalists from The Duke of Wellington and Castle Eden Inn. Great food should be complemented by good drink, whether that is wine or beer. Once again, the North East has some great wine suppliers supplying fine wines and lesser known boutique products from small estates. Alongside with this, we have some superb regional micro breweries producing great cask and bottled ales.

The North East is now blessed with cuisines from around the world served by a diverse range of chefs and restaurants. And while the region is rightly proud of its heritage and regional produce we should make no apology for using the best ingredients and artisan products from wherever they come, nationally or internationally.

Enjoy this book, but more importantly, get out there and relish the North East.

Terry Laybourne

010 BARRASFORD ARMS

Hexham, Northumberland NE48 4AA

01434 681 237
www.barrasfordarms.co.uk

Family run with a fine, friendly, supporting team this is a small hotel with a large following, which has been nestling under the ramparts of Haughton Castle since 1887. Its patrons enjoy succulent fare, reflecting the underlying ethos of ensuring meals are a balance of quality and quantity. Beer or cocktails in front of a blazing fire, a prelude to anything from flambé to fricassee and fine wines from a varied but robust cellar. With the wines, garnered from all corners of the world, there is an emphasis on France. The chef is strenuous in supporting local producers but imparting subtle French influence and flavours to the absorbing menu.

Tony Binks, proprietor and head chef, is a pupil of Albert Roux and now a master in his own right, liberally passing on his own knowledge to younger aspirants. Tony has put the hotel firmly on the epicurean map. He receives solid support from villagers, the hunting fraternity and fishing fanatics on the adjacent North Tyne.

He has honed his culinary skills by working through the entire spectrum of kitchens but realises that there are still stones to be turned and tricks to be learned. Though the hub of this charming hideaway is the interaction of the bar, kitchen and dining rooms. There are eight en suite bedrooms, many with stunning views across the river to the castle, but all providing comfort to recover from the river, a walk or a surfeit of the delicacies downstairs.

Adherents of The Barrasford Arms have failed to keep this gem a secret. So be sure to come along and try our breakfast, lunch or dinner.

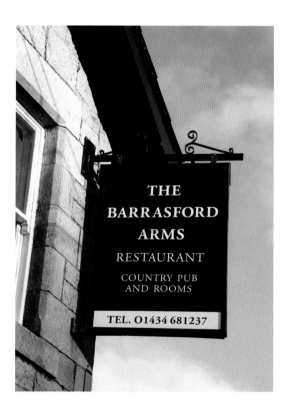

THE BARRASFORD ARMS
RESTAURANT
COUNTRY PUB AND ROOMS

TEL. 01434 681237

A pupil of Albert Roux and now a master in his own right, liberally passing on his own knowledge to younger aspirants, Tony Binks has put the hotel firmly on the epicurean map.

WILD RABBIT LOIN SALAD, APPLE & CIDER SYRUP

SERVES 4

Montagny
1er Cru- Olivier Leflaive

Ingredients

Rabbit

4 wild rabbit loins
10ml olive oil
1 sprig of rosemary
½ clove garlic
mixed baby leaf salad
2 Granny Smiths apples
seasoning

Dressing

25ml rapeseed oil
12ml Cider vinegar
seasoning

Apple Sauce

100g Bramley apples (peeled and chopped)
40g caster sugar
25ml cider vinegar
25g butter

Cider Syrup

250ml dry cider
100g sugar
pinch mixed spice

Method

For the rabbit

Marinade rabbit loins in olive oil, rosemary and chopped garlic, gently seal in a non stick frying pan. Season, cook until just pink. Let the meat rest, slice when required.

For the dressing

Whisk rapeseed oil into cider vinegar and season gently. Dress salad leaves and add a little thinly sliced apple.

For the cider syrup

Dissolve the sugar in the cider and add the mixed spice. Simmer until reduced to a syrup. Cool and serve.

For the apple sauce

Put the apples, sugar, cider vinegar and butter into a microwave dish and cook on full power for 3 minutes until apple pulps. Purée with stick blender.

To serve

Assemble as in the picture.

COLDINGHAM MOOR WILD BOAR SADDLE, SAVOURY DUCKS, CALVADOS, AGEN PRUNES AND APPLE SAUCE

SERVES 4

Rioja Reserva
Solar de Samaniego

Ingredients

Wild Boar

1 x 400g bone rack wild boar
400g boar eye loin
sage and parsley (chopped)
500ml stock made from bones and trimmings
100ml port
50g butter

Savoury Ducks

200g boar belly trimmings
50g kidney, 50g liver
25g fresh white bread crumbs
25g shallots (chopped)
100g pigs caul
nutmeg
salt and pepper

Apple Sauce

100g Bramley apples (chopped and peeled)
40g caster sugar
25ml cider vinegar
25g butter

Glazed Agen Prunes and Apple

8 Agen prunes
2 Granny Smith apples
50ml Calvados
50g caster sugar
75g butter
50ml cider

Cabbage Balls

1 small Savoy cabbage
50g butter
salt and pepper

Fondant Potato

4 x size 60 (370g) baking potatoes
150g hard butter
salt and pepper

Method

For the wild boar rack

Score the wild boar, brush with oil, season with salt & pepper. Place on cooling wire and roast in a shallow roasting tin at 200°C until the core temperature is 65°C. Allow to rest.

For the wild boar eye loin

Season the loin with salt and pepper. Seal in hot oil and butter and brown all sides. Cook in a hot oven at 180°C until the core temperature is 65°C. Allow to rest.

For the savoury duck

Mince belly, liver and trimmed kidney through fine holes of a mincer. Gently cook the chopped shallots in a little butter. Then allow to cool. Add breadcrumbs, chopped herbs and season with salt, pepper and nutmeg. Divide into four balls and wrap in pigs caul. Place in a lightly buttered oven dish, covered 2/3 with bone stock. Gently braise in oven at 140°C for 45 minutes. Remember to retain the cooking liquor.

For the apple sauce

Put all ingredients into a microwave dish and cook on full power for 3 minutes until the apple pulps. Purée with stick blender.

For the glazed agen prunes and apple

Melt butter in a thick bottomed pan, add turned apple, prunes and add sugar. Cook until it starts to melt. Add sugar, cider and calvados. Lower the heat and cook until apple is tender and reduced to syrup.

For the stuffed cabbage

Remove the outer leaves and de-vein, then shred the remaining cabbage and blanch in salted boiling water. Drain when cooked, sauté the shredded cabbage in melted butter and season. Form four cabbage balls. Wrap each with outer leaf then brush with butter.

For the fondant potato

Slice the hard butter and place in a thick bottomed pan. Add potatoes and heat until butter starts to foam, cover 2/3 with water and with greaseproof paper and cook until potatoes are tender and glazed.

For the sauce

Reduce remaining stock and liquor from savoury ducks, add port, butter and serve.

To serve

Assemble as in the picture.

RHUBARB AND CUSTARD SHORTBREAD

SERVES 4

Pinot Noir 2006, red harvest
California

Ingredients

Rhubarb

300g rhubarb sticks
25g melted butter
100g sugar
100ml Grenadine
1 blood orange

Custard

6 egg yolks
125g caster sugar
30g plain flour
10g custard powder
500ml milk
1 vanilla pod (split)
1 leaf of gelatine

Shortbread

200g plain flour
200g unsalted butter
100g caster sugar
100g cornflour
caster sugar for dusting

Method

For the rhubarb

Trim and wash the rhubarb then cut into equal lengths, approx 8cm. Three to four pieces per portion. Brush an ovenproof dish with the melted butter and sprinkle with the sugar. Lay the rhubarb sticks in the dish but do not overlap. Pour the grenadine, juice and zest of an orange over the rhubarb, cover with foil and bake in the oven at 180°C for approx 20 minutes. The rhubarb should be tender and intact. Allow to cool.

For the custard

Place egg yolks and 1/3 of the sugar in a bowl. Whisk until pale until it forms a light ribbon. Sift in flour and custard powder and mix well. Combine milk, remaining sugar and the split vanilla pod in a saucepan and bring to the boil. As soon as the mixture bubbles, pour 1/3 into egg mixture stirring constantly. Pour mixture back into the pan over a gentle heat, keep stirring. Boil for 2 minutes and add the soaked gelatine leaf. Make sure this dissolves. Pour into container and allow to cool.

For the shortbread

Add flour, butter and cornflour into a mixing machine using a paddle on slow speed until the butter and flour crumbs. Add sugar and increase speed until a firm dough is formed. Wrap in clingfilm and allow to rest in a refrigerator for 20 minutes. Turn out into floured work surface and roll out to approx 4mm thick and cut into eight rectangles, approx 3 x 8 cm. Cook on baking parchment paper for 12 minutes at 180°C. Once cooked, dust with caster sugar.

To serve

Assemble as in the picture.

Lots of Love

BATTLESTEADS

Richard & Dee xx

Wark on Tyne nr Hexham, Northumberland NE48 3LS

01434 230 209
www.battlesteads.com

Great Hospitality Doesn't Need To Cost The Earth.

Anyone who appreciates the finer things in life and is looking for great value will love Battlesteads pub/hotel in Wark, near Hexham, which is renowned for its superb food, warm and welcoming hospitality and outstanding 'green' credentials. Nestled in the heart of stunning Hadrian's Wall country, Battlesteads has much to offer the discerning guest: a cosy bar and lounge area with five real ales on hand pump, a main restaurant area with its dark wood furnishings and low lighting, and a conservatory with views of the walled garden; a great vantage point for eyeing the array of wildlife. It also has 17 well-appointed en-suite rooms.

Owners Richard and Dee Slade have won several prestigious awards from the likes of VisitEngland and Green Tourism Business Scheme for the outstanding service at Battlesteads and the hotel's incredible strides towards sustainable tourism. It was also voted 2010 Great British Pub of the Year by the Morning Advertiser pub trade magazine.

Green highlights include the 100% carbon-neutral biomass boiler providing heating and hot water to the entire hotel, a complete rainwater harvesting and reuse system and an extensive programme of energy-saving initiatives and installations.

Most of the food served in the 80-seater restaurant is either grown on-site in the two acre gardens and two polytunnels or sourced from independent artisan producers within 25 miles of the village. Chef Eddie promises field to plate in four hours and everything grown on-site is free from artificial fertilisers and herbicides.

Battlesteads is heaven on earth for guests with a sweet tooth as dessert chef and chocolatier Dee Slade tempts the tastebuds with her award-winning masterpieces!

Breakfast at Battlesteads is a treat in itself. What with low salt smoked haddock and kippers, black pudding made on-site by chef Eddie Shilton plus locally made award-winning preserves, it's a feast to behold and sets guests up for their day ahead

SMOKEY GAME AND CHESTNUT SOUP

SERVES 8-10

Huia Marlborough
Pinot Noir

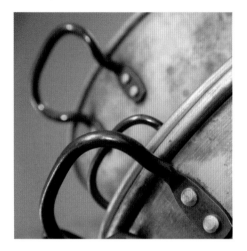

Ingredients

1 large potato (peeled and diced)
500g cooked chestnuts (peeled and chopped)
5 rashers of smoked pancetta
1 medium carrot (peeled and diced)
1 medium onion (finely chopped)
2 celery sticks (finely chopped)
300g piece of venison loin or fillet
any other scraps of game
2.5 litres of game stock (made from venison bones or any game carcasses)
small handful of fresh thyme (finely chopped)

Method

Lay the pancetta rashers over the venison loin.

In a medium oven (150°C or Gas Mark 5) roast the meat until the pancetta is browned and all the fat has separated.

Use the fat to cook the carrots, potato, onion and celery for 5 minutes without colouring.

Add the chestnuts and any cooked scraps of game into the vegetables.

Cover with the stock and add the fresh thyme then cover the pan and simmer gently for 40 minutes.

Meanwhile slice the venison finely and then chop into small pieces.

Chop the crisp pancetta into small pieces.

Remove 60% of the solids from the pan and blitz to a puree, then add back into the pan.

Add the chopped venison and pancetta, stir and serve garnished with fresh thyme.

Season to taste.

To serve

Assemble as in the picture.

Chef's tip

This is a really good way of using up the carcass, bones and scraps from venison, pheasant, partridge and grouse. Talk to your game dealer and I'm sure he'd let you have some bones and carcasses for free! Using venison loin adds a touch of luxury.

WILD BASS, BROWN SHRIMP AND LENTILS WITH WHITE ONION CREAM

SERVES 4

Kleine Rust Fair Trade
Chenin Sauvignon

Ingredients

4 wild bass fillets
rapeseed oil
salt and freshly ground black pepper

Lentils

1 large knob of butter
250g puy or brown lentils (soaked and picked)
1 carrot (finely diced)
1 celery stick (finely diced)
4 cloves garlic (finely chopped)
½ onion (finely chopped)
250 ml white wine
1 ¼ litres chicken or vegetable stock
75g brown shrimps or prawns
Black kale (shredded)

White Onion Cream

115g butter
2 large onions (finely chopped)

Method

For the lentils

Melt the butter in a large saucepan and soften the garlic, onion, celery and carrot.

Add the lentils and stir to coat with the butter.

Add the white wine and stock, cover and cook gently for 20 to 25 minutes (until cooked but still slightly firm) adding more stock if needed.

Stir in the shredded black kale, shrimps or prawns and keep warm.

For the white onion cream

Melt 115g of butter in a non stick pan and add the chopped onions. Cook very slowly and gently until the onions are soft and slightly coloured.

Purée the onions, add salt and pepper to taste.

For wild bass fillets

Pre heat a skillet or non stick sauté pan

Brush the skin of the wild bass with a little rapeseed oil and season.

Place skin side down onto the skillet, for 4 minutes, turn over and take off the heat.

To serve

Place the lentils in the centre of the plate, spoon the warm white onion cream around the risotto and top with the wild bass fillets.

BLOOD ORANGE, HAZELNUT AND TREACLE TART

SERVES 6-8

The Stump Jump Sticky Chardonnay

Method

For the sweet pastry

Add the icing sugar to the flour and stir to blend.

Rub the butter into the flour until the texture is similar to a crumble mixture.

Add water and fold in lightly until the pastry forms and binds.

Wrap in clingfilm and refrigerate for 1 hour.

Pre heat the oven to 200°C, 400F or Gas Mark 6.

Roll out the pastry to line a 9 inch flan ring (loose bottomed).

Blind bake for 10 to 15 minutes until set.

For the filling

Melt the butter and syrup together.

Add all the other ingredients in the melted mixture.

Pour into the tart case.

Bake in the oven at 180°C, 350F or Gas Mark 4 for 15 to 20 minutes.

To serve

Assemble as in the picture.

Ingredients

Filling

50g unsalted butter
130g golden syrup
225g fresh brioche (made into breadcrumbs)
1 blood orange (finely grated zest and juice)
25g toasted hazelnuts (finely chopped without skin)

Sweet Pastry

175g unsalted butter
240g plain flour
50g sifted icing sugar
60ml cold water

030
BLACKFRIARS RESTAURANT & BANQUET HALL

Friars Street, Newcastle NE1 4XN

0191 261 5945
www.blackfriarsrestaurant.co.uk

Established in 1239 as a Dominican friary, Blackfriars has had a long and turbulent history that included a spell as a hostel to accommodate nobles and royals such as Kings Henry III and Edward III. As a former friary in commercial use today, it is undoubtedly time-enduring and unique. Blackfriars has become one of the city's most recognised restaurants and is now regarded as a local institution.

In addition to the main restaurant, the splendour of Blackfriars' ornate medieval Banquet Hall has been brought back to life following years of painstaking and meticulous research and restoration. The celebrated venue King Edward III used for receiving royal Scot, Edward Balliol, in 1334, boasts authentic and bespoke banners, chandeliers, wall coverings, stained-glass windows, reclaimed wooden screens, large oak communal dining tables and matching chairs, all created by local craftsmen.

The Banquet Hall regularly plays host to authentic medieval banquets with pottages, smoked meats served on bread trenchers, roast mutton, goose, suckling pygge and pastries served on the large, candle-lit communal tables by costumed staff and real medieval entertainment!

The hall, which also has its own separate kitchen and bar, accommodates 50 guests and is the perfect venue for corporate and private functions, special occasions and weddings.

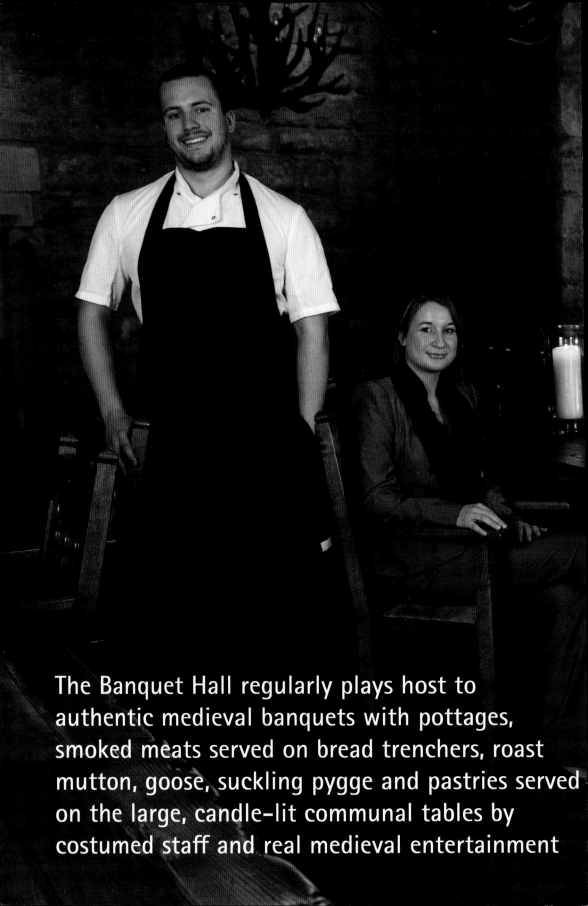

The Banquet Hall regularly plays host to authentic medieval banquets with pottages, smoked meats served on bread trenchers, roast mutton, goose, suckling pygge and pastries served on the large, candle-lit communal tables by costumed staff and real medieval entertainment

SMOKED MEATS ON BREAD TRENCHERS, FRUIT FROM THE CRUSADES CHUTNEY

SERVES 12

 Cherry-flavoured Trappist beer

Ingredients

Barley Bread Trencheurs

500g strong wholemeal flour
225g Northumberland barley flour
25g Crussaders rice flour
½ tbsp sea salt
15g fresh bakers yeast
60ml Newcastle Brown Ale
425ml warm water
2tsp Chainbridge clear honey

Smoked Meats

2 breasts from free-range chicken, Mallard or other wild duck

Pork, Pistachio and Apricot Terrine

600g fatty pork (minced)
75g dried apricots (chopped)
50g pistachios
400g streaky bacon
200g fresh pork liver
2 tbsp fresh flatleaf parsley (finely chopped)
Sea salt and freshly ground black pepper

Fruit from the Crusades Chutney

2 tsp rapeseed oil
1 red onion (sliced)
2 red chillies (finely chopped)
600g fruit from the Crusades (1 small pineapple if available, peeled, core removed, finely chopped)
1 lime (juice only)
100ml apple vinegar
100g cane sugar

Method

From barley bread trencheurs

Form dough, knead until elastic, cover and leave until doubled in size.

Punch down, halve and shape into 2 round loafs.

Cover with cloth and leave in a warm place until risen.

Bake at 230°C for 25 minutes until base sounds hollow when tapped underneath.

For the smoked meats

Smoke on top of apple wood, cool and thinly slice.

For the pork, pistachio and apricot terrine

Preheat the oven to 160°C.

Mix ingredients.

Place the rashers of streaky bacon along the edge of a loaf tin, overlapping the bacon in the base a little leaving about 3cm of the rashers draping over the sides of the tin.

Layer ingredients into tin and when the tin is full, fold over the draping bacon to cover the filling.

Place the loaf tin into a bain-marie that is half full of hot water and place into the oven to cook for about 1¼ - 1½ hours, or until completely cooked through.

Remove the loaf tin from the oven and allow to cool completely before placing in the fridge to chill.

For the chutney

Heat the oil in a pan, then fry the onion and chillies for 2-3 minutes until softened.

Add the pineapple, lime juice, cider vinegar and sugar and bring to the boil.

Reduce the heat and simmer for 15 minutes, then remove from the heat and leave to cool.

To serve

Serve in 'messes' of four diners which should include one dish of each of the meats/terrines and one pot of chutney plus one loaf of trenchers and one pot of ale.

ROAST SUCKLING PYGGE

SERVES 20-30

🍷 *Strong cider or red Beaujolais if merchants have some*

Ingredients

Suckling Pygge

10 to 15kg suckling pygge

Drawn Beans

450g garden broad beans
2 cloves garlic
2 large onions
large pinch saffron
rapeseed oil/lard
sprinkle of cane sugar
sprinkle of cinnamon

Compost

100g garden radishes
225g parsnips (scraped and cut into large chunks)
225g turnips (scraped and cut into large chunks)
225g cabbage (coarsely chopped)
3 pears (stalks removed)
1 tbs salt
300ml white wine
300ml white wine vinegar
50g raisins
¼ tsp ground cinnamon
¼ tsp aniseed
¼ tsp fennel seed
large pinch saffron
½ tsp ground mustard

Method

For the suckling pygge

Wash, dry, season and stuff with garlic and sage.

Oil up and oven or spit roast at 45 minutes per kilo until juices run clear.

Rest for 30 minutes.

Carve and serve.

For the drawn beans

Simmer beans for 25 minutes until they burst, then drain.

Fry beans, onion and garlic in oil or lard for 10 minutes.

Pour into dish and sprinkle with sugar and cinnamon.

For the compost

Simmer vegetables for 10 minutes.

Add pears and simmer for a further 10 minutes.

Drain, pat dry and sprinkle with salt. Leave overnight.

In the morning, wipe salt from vegetables and pears.

Place in a stoneware jar with spiced wine vinegar.

Leave for a week before using.

To serve

Wait for your carver to slice the meat and cut into bite-sized pieces to be eaten with your left hand. Again serve in 'messes' of four diners with one dish of accompanying vegetables per mess.

FRIED FIG PASTIES

SERVES 12

 Lindisfarne Mead

Method

Combine filling, including the egg yolk.

Lightly beat egg white and brush 1 sheet of pastry, then cut into strips 7cm wide.

Put a small spoonful of mixture at one end of the pastry strip then roll up, pinch ends closed.

Continue until all pastry and mixture has been used up.

Deep fry in lard.

Baste in warm honey before serving.

To serve

Serve in the 'messes' of four diners, with one pot of mead or hypocras (spiced sweet wine) per mess.

Chef's tip

Set in Wyte grece (lard) over a the fire in a chaufour (cauldron) and fry till done.

Ingredients

450g dried figs (soaked, drained and minced)
(Also make sure you reserve the liquor)
Powder fort (Medieval recipe made from 1/8 tsp
each of ground ginger, cloves and black pepper)
pinch saffron soaked in fig liquor
1/4 tsp salt
1 egg
6 sheets of filo pastry
lard
225ml warmed Chainbridge honey

040
BOUCHON BISTROT

4-6 Gilesgate, Hexham, Northumberland NE46 3NJ

01434 609 943
www.bouchonbistrot.co.uk

Bouchon brings a little corner of rural France to Northumberland. French-owned and run, this is the classic country bistrot (hence the classic French spelling, with a 't') where you can close your eyes and the tastes, smells and sounds of France are yours. Our style is traditional; our signature menus features classics such as Escargots with Garlic and Parsley Butter, Pork Rillettes, Simply Roasted Chicken carved at the table and Brittany Fish Market Stew. Our classic desserts include Clafoutis aux Cerises, Tarte Tatin aux Pommes, Crème Caramel and Crêpes Suzettes.

Our French onion soup represents the essence of France in a single bowl; a simple and traditional dish prepared, like all our food, expertly, confidently and with respect for every ingredient.

Our dishes, like our restaurant, are fresh and uncomplicated, created from the finest produce and served simply and in season in the traditional French country way.

Long, laid-back lunches, big family dinners or romantic dining a deux: our18th Century home in the heart of Hexham's historic leather tanning and merchants' quarter is warm and intimate; a little corner of France in the Tyne Valley.

Alors Bon Appétit!

Gregory Bureau, owner

Our dishes, like our restaurant, are fresh and uncomplicated, created from the finest produce and served simply and in season in the traditional French country way

TERRINE DE FOIE GRAS WITH HOMEMADE TOASTED BRIOCHE

SERVES 4

🍷 *Savennières "Clos du Papillon" 2007 Domaine des Baumard*

Method

Remove the vein and the blood of the lobe with a small paring knife, then season with the salt and pepper and then sugar the foie gras on the entire surface.

Marinate the lobe with the 3 alcohols for 12 hours.

Put the lobe in a terrine dish, and cook for 45 minutes at 90°C.

Leave in the fridge for at least 1 day in order to mature before eating.

To serve

Serve slices of foie gras at room temperature, with freshly toasted brioche, and a sauternes jelly.

Bon Appétit!

Chef's tips

For the Foie Gras: leave the foie gras lobe for 12 hours in 50% milk 50% water. It will give you a neater colour for the final result.

Ingredients

1 lobe of foie gras, of the best quality possible
25ml port
25ml cognac
25ml Muscat wine
7g salt
2.5g white pepper
1 pinch of sugar

BRITTANY FISH MARKET STEW

SERVES 4

*Collioure Blanc 2009
from Abbe Rous*

Ingredients

Fish

1 lobster
1 John Dory
1 grey mullet

Lobster Bisque

the shell from the lobster
1 small carrot
1 banana shallot
1 small onion
¼ leek (white part only)
1 tsp of orange zest
2 garlic cloves
25ml of Ricard or Pernod
1 tbsp tomato purée
1 Bouquet Garni
100ml Cognac
150ml Muscadet
1 pinch of fresh saffron
knob of butter

Vegetables

6 baby potatoes
2 celery sticks
2 carrots
150g white mushrooms

Method

For the lobster and sauce

Blanch the Lobster for 4 minutes in a "Court Bouillon" (aromated water) then remove the flesh from the shell and put aside for later.

Cook the shell in olive oil until the bottom of the lobster becomes nicely brown, and then remove the shell, also discarding as much fat as possible. Add a knob of butter, all the vegetables cut in "brunoise" (small dices) and the tomato purée. Sweat off the vegetables for 4 to 5 minutes on a medium heat, then add the Lobster shell. Deglaze with the Cognac and flame it. Reduce until dry and add the Muscadet then boil for 4 to 5 minutes to get rid of the acidity. Add 1 litre of water, add the bouquet garni, 2 gloves of garlic, the Ricard and the orange zest.

Simmer for 45 minutes, blitz in a food processor and pass the mixture through a thin chinois and reserve.

For the vegetables

Dice the carrots and cook them in salted water until tender but with a bit of a bite; do the same with the celery. Peel your potatoes and cook them in water with lemon juice and saffron. Pan fry the mushrooms in butter until golden brown.

For the fish

Cut your fish to portions making sure there are no bones left. Pan fry your fish fillets in a non-stick pan with olive oil at a very high temperature. The fillets must get a nice colour but remain undercooked in the middle.

To finish the dish, put all the components in with the sauce and cook for a further 7 minutes. Place the vegetables and the fishes in a serving bowl, reduce the sauce by half and emulsify with butter.

To serve

Pour the sauce over the fish and vegetables. Et voila!!

Chef's tip

Dry the lobster shell in the oven, then cut them and blitz to a powder in a food processor. Sprinkle the powder in the sauce to enhance the flavours.

MOUSSE AU CHOCOLAT
WITH MACARONS À LA VANILLE

SERVES 4

*Vouvray Moelleux 2005 "Le Haut Lieu" from
Gaston Huet or Chateau Coutet (Sauternes)*

Ingredients

Mousse au chocolat

150g dark chocolate
80g butter
2 egg yolks
3 egg whites (2 x 80g)
25g sugar

Macarons à la Vanille

(around 40 macarons)
200g ground almonds
200g icing sugar
2 x 80g egg whites
½ vanilla pod

Sugar Syrup

200g sugar
25ml water

Method

For the macarons

Mix the ground almonds and icing sugar, then pass it through a sieve. Mix it with 80g of egg white (half of the 3 egg whites) in order to create a paste. Scrape the vanilla pod in the mix.

Make the sugar syrup and set aside.

Create a meringue with the other remaining 80g of egg white, mixing it slowly initially, then add the sugar syrup gently.

With a soft spatula, incorporate ⅓ of the meringue into the almond paste in order to soften it up, then add the rest of the meringue to the mix.

Use a piping bag with a 8mm nozzle, pipe the mix onto a grease proof-paper, shaping into little balls (the size of a nut). Leave the balls to "crust" for around 30 minutes.

Meanwhile set your oven at 150°C; cook your macarons for 14 minutes, then leave to cool down.

Garnish your macarons with vanilla cream, chantilly or chocolate ganache.

For the mousse au chocolat

Melt the chocolate in a bain-marie, then add the butter. When the mix has melted, add the egg yolks very quickly.

Whisk the remaining egg whites until foamy; add the sugar and continue mixing until the egg whites begin to hold a shape.

Fold in a quarter of the whites with a wooden spatula just until incorporated, and then fold in the remaining whites.

Put the mix in dishes, and leave to set in the fridge for 6 hours.

To serve

Assemble as in the picture.

Chef's tip

When cooking the macarons leave the oven door slightly open towards the last 2 minutes of the cooking time.

050
THE BROAD CHARE

25 Broad Chare, Trinity Gardens, Newcastle upon Tyne NE1 3DQ

0191 211 2144
www.thebroadchare.co.uk

New to the city, The Broad Chare seems as though it's always been a part of Newcastle's historic Quayside.

That's no coincidence. It embraces the spirit of the best of a British pub featuring great English food, carefully selected craft beers and a warm, lived-in feel. The Broad Chare is a proper pub offering proper beer and proper food.

The comfy, atmospheric layout – a bar and snug downstairs, a dining room upstairs - suits the historic building in which it's housed. The style and hospitality is honest and unpretentious.

The Broad Chare is the latest venue in the expanding 21 Hospitality Group fronted by renowned chef and restaurateur Terry Laybourne. The pub is a creative partnership with Live Theatre, which owns the building. The pub, a seven-day a week operation, offers something new and fresh while also harnessing some of the best traditions of a British pub. The menu combines the best of traditional pub food with a big emphasis on seasonal, locally sourced produce.

For larger groups there is a range of 'feasting menus', where a roast rib of beef might be served in the middle of the table for a group followed by a steamed jam sponge or treacle pudding, with custard.

Focusing on real ale and craft beers, the pub offers its own bottled pale ale, The Writer's Block, brewed exclusively by Wylam Brewery to a unique recipe. A good range of wines by the glass is available along with an extensive selection of carefully chosen malt whiskies.

Bar snacks and simple meals are served on the ground floor. Meanwhile, the main dining area upstairs, offers hearty, wholesome food.

Head Chef Chris Eagle

Focusing on real ale and craft beers, the pub offers its own bottled pale ale, The Writer's Block, brewed exclusively by Wylam Brewery to a unique recipe

SCOTCH EGG WITH CAPER MAYONNAISE

SERVES 4 AS A BAR SNACK

*The Writer's Block
(bottled pale ale)*

Ingredients

4 very fresh eggs
150g best quality pork sausage meat
2tbsp onion (finely chopped)
1tbsp soft butter
1 pinch rosemary (finely chopped)
1 pinch thyme (finely chopped)
1 pinch sage (finely chopped)
150g Haggis
salt and milled black
pepper
plain flour
1 hen's egg
100ml milk
300g dry breadcrumbs
oil for deep frying
caper mayonnaise

Method

Cook the eggs in boiling salted water for 7 minutes, then chill in iced water.

Carefully remove the shells and reserve the eggs in the refrigerator.

Cook the onion in butter for 4-5 minutes until soft but without colour, stirring in the chopped herbs and remove from the heat.

Transfer to a plate and allow to cool.

When thoroughly cooled mix the onion into the sausage meat along with the haggis. Season with salt and pepper.

Divide into 5 even portions and flatten each between two sheets of clingfilm until around 5mm thick.

Dry the eggs on a clean cloth and place an egg into the centre of each disk of sausage meat.

Wrap the eggs completely, ensuring that the eggs are fully covered.

Beat the hen's egg together with the milk. Roll the wrapped eggs in flour, then add the egg/milk mixture and then finally roll in the dried breadcrumbs.

Transfer to a clean tray, lined with greaseproof paper.

To serve

Deep fry at 180°C until golden. Cut in half and serve immediately with caper mayonnaise on the side.

range of tasty bar snacks from oysters, pork crackling to scotch eggs

7 HOUR SHOULDER OF LAMB

SERVES 5-6

Shiraz from Chile

Ingredients

2.5kg lamb shoulder on the bone
sea salt
milled black pepper
olive oil
2 onions (peeled and cut into large chunks)
1 head garlic (unpeeled, cut in half through the equator)
1 sprig rosemary
1 large sprig thyme
400ml dry white wine
400ml or more lamb or chicken stock

Method

Set the oven on as low a temperature as possible (ideally around 80°C).

Warm a heavy, cast iron roasting tray over a medium heat with 5tbsp olive oil.

Season the lamb shoulder generously with salt and pepper.

Colour the lamb gently on all sides in the roasting tray.

Scatter the onions and garlic around and stir to coat them with oil.

Continue cooking until nicely caramelised.

Remove the lamb from the tray, add the herbs and pour in the wine.

Bring to a boil, scraping the base of the tray to release any sediment.

Return the shoulder to the tray and cover tightly with a double thickness of aluminium foil.

Place in the low oven and cook for 2 hours or so.

Remove the foil and add lamb stock.

Return to the oven and continue cooking, basting every now and again with the stock, adding a little more as and when needed.

After 7 hours the lamb should be incredibly tender and the surface sticky and glazed from the reduced stock.

Place the roasting dish in the centre of the table, on a trivet, along with a large pair of tongs for pulling the meat apart.

To serve

Potato hotpot or creamy potato gratin make great accompaniments along with a large bowl of buttery, steamed greens.

LEMON PUDDLE PUDDING

SERVES 6

Method

Grate the zest from the lemons then squeeze the juice.

Cream the butter and sugar until light and fluffy.

Carefully beat in the egg yolks.

Sift in the flour and fold through.

Carefully fold in the milk and lemon juice.

Whisk the egg white to soft peaks and carefully fold into the mixture also.

Spoon into a buttered and floured pie dish.

Sit the pie dish in a large deep roasting tray and fill with 1½" of hot water.

Bake in the oven at 180°C for 40 – 45 minutes until golden and just firm to the touch.

Remove and allow to cool for 5 minutes before serving.

To serve

Assemble as in the picture.

Ingredients

2 lemons
100g butter
230g sugar
3 small eggs (separated)
70g plain flour
155ml full fat milk

060
CASTLE EDEN INN

Stockton Road, Castle Eden, Hartlepool, Cleveland TS27 4SD

01429 835 137
www.castleedeninn.com

The Castle Eden Inn is a traditional coaching inn which can be dated back to Dick Turpin where legend has it he was actually chained up outside the Inn, before being taken to York to be executed. The Inn has a fantastic history and since being transformed in 2009, it is beginning to relive the glory days, which once made it the flagship for the area.

Situated in the picturesque village of Castle Eden, the Castle Eden Inn been lovingly refurbished and now boasts one of the best restaurants within the area receiving excellent reviews from the media and customers alike.

Under the guidance of Masterchef finalist and Head Chef David Coulson, the emphasis has been switched to locally sourced produce; focused simplicity resulting in complex and beautiful flavours descending upon the customers palate. David is insistent on only using the best local suppliers, building relationships with these suppliers so we actually have produce grown to David's own requirements.

The Castle Eden Inn is a wonderful place to indulge whether it is a traditional lunch or a venture to experience the comprehensive menu David has created. Order from one of the many daily specials which involve produce that has been delivered within hours. What we like to refer to as complex simplicity leads to fantastic flavours that entice the customer and take them on an exquisite journey through starter, mains and desserts. The exceptional food is accompanied by a large range of real ales, wines, champagnes, spirits and now a selection of cocktails made using fresh fruit, and an extensive beer garden.

The Castle Eden Inn is open 7 days a week and makes for a memorable visit, and a place to relax, socialise and enjoy David and his team's creations. Be sure to ask what Ermelito the patisserie chef has on offer; from the most beautiful take on a traditional apple crumble as seen later in the book to a wide selection of homemade ice creams, which can include some interesting flavours such as blue cheese!

Under the guidance of Masterchef finalist and Head Chef David Coulson, the emphasis has been switched to locally sourced produce; focused simplicity resulting in complex and beautiful flavours descending upon the customers palate

HADDOCK, BLACK PUDDING AND EGG

SERVES 4

🍷 *Muscadet Sèvre et Maine Sur Lie, Guillaume Charpentier Loire, France*

Ingredients

2 fillets of Hodgsons smoked haddock (cut into 4, reserve the scrap for the haddock mousse)

4 quails eggs

Doreen of black pudding

200g dry mashed (riced) potato

100ml white wine reduced

100ml double cream

50g chives (chopepd)

40g tomato concasse

200g chard

2 eggs

50g Northumberland smoked cheese

Method

For the croquette

First mould the croquette, mix 200g of the Doreen black pudding with the dry mash and mould.

Cut into inch cylinders and panne.

Keep in the fridge until frying.

For the haddock mousse

In a magi mix blend the scrap from the haddock with a splash of double cream and an egg yolk, reserve in the fridge.

For the quails eggs

In boiling salted water, cook the quails eggs for 2 minutes and 10 seconds exactly, then immediately put into iced water. Peel them and coat in the haddock mousse and then panne??

For the sauce

Reduce the wine to a tablespoon then add cream and reduce to sauce consistency and add grated Northumberland Smoked Cheese. Add the chives and tomato concasse just before serving.

For the haddock

Put a knob of butter on the haddock and grill for 2 minutes.

To assemble

In a hot pan add a knob of butter and a splash of oil and sauté the spinach. Season with salt and white pepper.

Fry the croquette and quails eggs.

To serve

Assemble as in the picture.

FILLET OF NEASHAM BEEF, ROOT VEGETABLES, CLAPSHOT PURÉE AND BRAISED CHEEK

SERVES 4

🍷 A'Amarone,
Alpha Zeta Veneto Italy

Ingredients

1 cut of Tournedos fillet (rolled in clingfilm and cut into 4)
2 beef cheeks
1kg carrots
1kg swede
4 leeks
2 onions
3 beetroot
2 sticks of celery
black pepper
1 butter
sprigs of rosemary and thyme
2 kg chicken stock (white)
1 bottle of red wine (preferable Barolo)
5 parsnips
1 celeriac
200g double cream
seasoning
200g charlotte potatoes

Method

A day in advance marinate the beef cheeks in carrot, leek, celery, onions, thyme, rosemary, garlic, bay, black pepper corns and a bottle of red wine preferably Barolo.

After 24 hours remove the cheeks. Pat dry and seal in a very hot pan, put back in the marinate season then add chicken stock and cook for 8 hours at 160°C. The liquor should have taken on a nice syrupy sauce consistency.

For the purée

Peel and cut 200g of swede and 200g of carrot, cover with white chicken stock and season. Cook until nearly dry and cover with another layer of chicken stock and reduce again. Add 100g of butter and liquidise until smooth and glossy.

For the dauphinose

Thinly slice the carrot, swede, parsnip, celeriac, beetroot and potato on a mandolin. Layer up 9 dauphinose with a layer of veg between each layer of potato, not forgetting to season sporadically.

Infuse the cream with garlic, thyme and rosemary. After simmering pass over the dauphinoise and cook at 150°C for 1 minute and 45 seconds.

Cook the fillet steak as you would like it cooked, in foaming butter, try adding garlic cloves and thyme.

When it is cooked to your satisfaction, it is important to rest it.

To serve

Enjoy whilst it's hot and assemble as in the picture.

CARAMEL APPLE CRUMBLE AND CUSTARD

SERVES 4-6

Moscatel, Bodega de Sarria, 15 % abv Navarra Spain

Ingredients

Apple Compote

juice of 1 lemon
2 kg Bramley apples
300g caster sugar
50g unsalted butter
2 vanilla pods

Crumble

100g plain flour
50g granulated sugar
pinch of cinnamon
50g unsalted butter
50g toasted hazelnuts (lightly crushed)

Caramel Custard

165g caster sugar
150ml double cream
375ml whole milk
1 vanilla pod
25g corn flour
4 large egg yolks

Method

For the custard

Caramelize 100g of the sugar and add 100ml of cream and mix then chill.

Infuse the milk with the vanilla pod. Meanwhile mix the rest of the sugar and corn flour in a large bowl. Add the egg yolks and beat to a smooth paste

Then add the infused milk, transfer to a clean pan and add the rest of the cream. Cook for 4-5 minutes until the corn flour is cooked.

For the apple compote

Peel and core the apples into acidulated water.

When done, pat them dry and put the chopped apples in a pan with sugar butter and vanilla pods.

Cook on a medium heat for 20 minutes.

For the crumble

In a food processer with a pulse function, put in the flour, sugar, cinnamon and butter. Pulse in the food processor until it resembles bread crumbs.

Remove to a bowl and stir in the hazelnuts.

In an oven proof dish assemble the crumble and cook for 25 minutes until its golden gas mark 6/200°C.

To serve

Eat when hot and enjoy your creation!

070
COLMANS

182 - 186 Ocean Road, South Shields, Tyne & Wear NE33 2JQ

0191 456 1202
www.colmansfishandchips.com

Colmans of South Shields has become a landmark seafood restaurant and a North East institution. This family business was founded in South Shields, Tyne & Wear, in 1926 with a culture of providing an excellent product combined with a first class service that continues to this day. Richard and Frances Ord are the current "stewards" of the Colman brand and they have, in recent years, added a level of sophistication and style to the business while never losing sight of the prime product...Traditional Fish and Chips!

The Colmans team are also enthusiastic advocates of offering their customers a variety of local and sustainably sourced fish and sea foods. The daily landed, hand peeled langoustines, lightly battered and deep fried, is a product that could easily be served in any fine dining restaurant and should not be missed when you visit Colmans!

Locally caught and prepared on the premises, crab, lobster, squid and many other sustainable species from the North Sea are also available every day at Colmans. However Traditional Fish and Chips remain the firm favourite. At Colmans, we believe we are blessed to be situated on the North East coast where we firmly believe we have access to some of the world's finest fish and seafoods.

Our team provide an experience at Colmans that makes you want to return again and again. They look forward to seeing you!

At Colmans, we believe we are blessed to be situated on the North East coast where we firmly believe we have access to some of the world's finest fish and seafoods

COLMANS STIR-FRIED SQUID WITH GARLIC, CHILLI AND TOASTED SESAME SEEDS

SERVES 4

 Gewurztraminer (Los Gansos) Chile or Ice Cold Peroni

Method

Clean the squid and then cut along one side of each pouch and open out flat. Score the inner side into a diamond pattern with the tip of a small sharp knife, and then cut into 5cm (2 inch) squares. Separate the tentacles if large and set both to one side.

Put six tablespoons of oil into a small pan, when hot add chopped chilli and garlic. Fry for a few seconds, then remove chilli and garlic onto kitchen paper to remove excess oil (do not let the garlic go brown as this will give it a bitter taste).

Heat a frying pan over a high heat, add sesame seeds and toast for a few seconds. Then remove from heat and set aside.

Heat a wok over a high heat until smoking, then add two tablespoons of the oil from the chilli and garlic and half the squid. Stir-fry for 2 minutes until lightly coloured. Tip onto a warm plate and repeat process with the rest of the squid.

To serve

Place the squid on a warm serving plate, add a couple of turns of salt and black pepper, sprinkle over garlic, chilli, toasted sesame seeds, spring onion and coriander and finally finish with a squeeze of fresh lime.

Chef's tip

Use locally caught Fresh Squid, it's delicious and sustainable.

Ingredients

750g fresh squid (unprepared)
2 medium hot red chillis (finely chopped)
3 garlic cloves (finely chopped)
1 tsp of toasted sesame seeds
3 spring onions (finely chopped)
2-3 fresh coriander sprigs (leaves and stalks, finely chopped)
6 tbs sunflower oil
1 lime
salt and black pepper

SIMPLE LOBSTER THERMIDOR

SERVES 2

Our House Champagne of course! Forget Brimont Premier Cru NV

Ingredients

750g lobster (cooked)
20g fresh grated parmesan

The sauce

30g butter
1 shallot (finely chopped)
284ml fresh fish stock
55ml white wine
100ml double cream
½ tsp English mustard
2 tbsp parsley (chopped)
½ lemon (juice only)
salt
freshly ground black pepper

Method

Cut the lobster in half and remove the meat from the claws and tail then leave to one side. Remove any meat from the head and set aside. Cut the meat into pieces and place back into the shell.

For the sauce

Put the butter in a pan, add the shallots and cook until softened. Add the stock, wine and double cream and bring to the boil. Reduce by half. Add the mustard, herbs, lemon juice and seasoning. Pre-heat the grill and spoon the sauce over the lobster meat. Sprinkle with the grated parmesan cheese. Place the lobster halves under a pre-heated grill for 3-4 minutes until golden brown.

To serve

Serve with a green salad and chunky chips.

Chef's tip

Use the meat from the head of the Lobster ,it doesn't look appetising but it will really make a difference to the sauce. Also stir in a little cold butter into the finished sauce for that professional finish!

COLMANS CRAB CAKES

SERVES 4

Gavi (Italy)
La Battistina.

Method

Place the crabmeat in a dish and check for any bits of shell, then scatter over the ingredients and mix very carefully with the crab, taking care not to break the crabmeat up too much.

Carefully form into 8 small cakes.

Refrigerate for one hour.

Heat a little olive oil in a pan until hot.

Carefully place in the cakes and cook for about 2-3 minutes on each side until golden brown.

To serve

Serve with a colourful salad.

Chef's tip

Add some brown crab meat with the mixture to create a more intense flavour.

Ingredients

450g freshly picked chunky white crabmeat
100g white breadcrumbs
4 tbsp mayonnaise
1 egg
1 tbsp Dijon mustard
1tbsp Worcestershire sauce
1 chilli (finely chopped)
chives and tarragon (chopped)
salt and freshly ground pepper
olive oil for frying
1 lemon

080
DABBAWAL

69-75 High Bridge Street, Newcastle upon Tyne NE1 6BX

www.dabbawal.com

Dabbawal brings you Indian food with an exciting twist. We're proud to be the North East's first Indian 'concept' restaurant and we invite you to experience the vibrant flavours of authentic Indian street food in the lively atmosphere and chic, urban interior of our Newcastle location. Our open kitchen will let you feel part of the scene, as grilled meats and hot fresh breads are cooked to perfection, in the tandoor before your eyes. "At Dabbawal, we're as passionate about our food as we are excited by the concept, so we pride ourselves on dishing up fresh and delicious food made with the very best ingredients we can source, because we know you can taste the difference", Jo Nessa, Business Development Manager. We're serving up a unique tapas-style sharing menu that lets our diners taste a variety of dishes in one sitting and caters perfectly to theatre-goers as well as late diners. Our menu also has lunchers and afternoon munchers in mind, with light, fresh dishes. We offer a selection of items from the grill, along with soups, salads and roomali wraps that won't slow you down. We want to make Indian food the answer to 'What's for lunch?'

If you're in the mood for something more, our big plates of curry and rice will hit the spot nicely. You'll be treated to a selection of classic curries along with a few surprises and signature dishes that we're proud to call our own. Dabbawal is more than a concept; we are the evolution of Indian food!

Our open kitchen will let you feel part of the scene, as grilled meats and hot fresh breads are cooked to perfection, in the tandoor before your eyes

DAHI BHALLA WITH DOSA

SERVES 4

🍷 *Gewurztraminer A.C. Alsace Cave de Turckeim
(France)*

Ingredients

Dosa (The Indian crepe)

recipe makes 8 dosas
115g basmati rice (rinsed)
70g split black lentils (urad dhal chilke)
¼ tsp fenugreek seeds
125ml water
salt to taste
30g ghee (melted)

Dahi Bhalla

100g split white lentils (urad dhal)
10g fresh ginger
1 onion
5g coriander leaves
curry leaves
salt to taste
1litre cooking oil
100g thick natural yogurt

Garnish

2g roasted cumin powder
1g red chilli powder

Method

For the dosa

Bring a pan of salted water to the boil, add the basmati rice and boil for 5 minutes, then drain. Put the rice, split black lentils and fenugreek seeds in a bowl and ensure all ingredients are immersed in water, leave to soak overnight.

The next day, drain the rice and lentils using a sieve. The rice and lentils need to be ground to a smooth paste, this can be done by using a food processor with 75ml of the water. Slowly add the remaining water.

Cover the bowl with a tea towel that has been soaked in hot water and wrung out then leave to ferment in a warm place or at room temperature for 5-6 hours until small bubbles appear all over the surface.

Stir the mixture and add as much extra water as necessary to get the consistency of single cream. Add salt to taste. Heat the flattest, largest pan you have over a high heat and then brush the surface with melted ghee.

Place a ladleful of this batter in the centre of the pan and spread the mixture out as thinly as possible, using the ladle in a circular motion. Flip the dosa over when it has started to crispen on the underside, cook for the same amount of time, leave on heat for longer to make crispier.

For the dahi bhalla

Wash the lentils and soak for 4 hours. Chop the onion, ginger, curry leaves and coriander leaves and mix together. Once the lentils have been soaked for 4 hours, drain them and grind into a smooth paste without adding water. This will be the batter for the vegetables.

When the batter has reached a thick consistency, mix in the vegetables, ensuring good coverage. Add salt to taste. Now you're ready to get cooking!

Pour the oil into a pan and place on a high heat. Make the battered vegetables into round ball shapes and fry once the oil has heated. Continue to stir until golden brown, then drain and keep to one side for approximately 20 minutes.

To serve

Prepare the dosa, yogurt and garnish. Place the vegetable balls onto the middle of the dosa, and loosely roll fajita-style. Serve up a generous helping of yogurt in a small dish and finally sprinkle the cumin and chilli powder over the top.

CHICKEN CHETTINAND

SERVES 4

 Sauvignon Blanc Jordan Estates
(South Africa)

Ingredients

300g fresh chicken fillet
10g garlic and ginger paste
5g mustard seeds
few curry leaves and coriander leaves

Marinade Paste

80ml coconut oil
salt to taste
5g cumin seeds
5g coriander seeds
5g star anise
5g clove
5g turmeric powder
1 cinnamon stick
grated coconut
1 whole red chilli
20g tamarind

Spiced Basmati Rice

225g basmati rice
1 baby aubergine (chopped)
1 medium tomato (chopped)
30g ghee or 2 tbsp vegetable oil
5 green cardamom pods (lightly cracked)
5 cloves
2 bay leaves
½ cinnamon stick
1tsp fennel seeds
450ml water
1 ½ tsp salt
2tbsp fresh coriander (chopped)
pepper to taste

Garnish

pinch of garam masala powder

Method

For the chicken

Begin by preparing the marinade paste by roasting the ingredients until they are a golden colour.

Once roasted, grind the spices into a smooth paste.

Wash and clean the chicken fillet and cube into small to medium size pieces.

Then marinate in the roasted masala paste and leave for 4-6 hours in the refrigerator.

Place the oil on the heat, at a medium-high temperature.

When the oil is ready, add the mustard seeds and curry leaves; this will cause the oil to crackle.

Add the garlic and ginger paste and roast for 5 minutes. Then add the chicken and cook for 15-20 minutes on a medium heat.

For the rice

Rinse the basmati rice several times until water runs clear, then leave to soak for 30 minutes. Drain and set aside until ready to cook.

Melt the ghee in a large saucepan with a tight-fitting lid over a medium-high heat.

Add the spices, stir for 30 seconds, and then add the aubergine, then stir for a further 60 seconds.

Stir the rice into the pan so the grains are coated with ghee.

Pour in the water, add the salt, and bring to the boil. Next, reduce the heat to as low as possible and cover the pan tightly.

Simmer, without lifting the lid, for 8 – 10 minutes until the grains are tender and all the liquid is absorbed.

Turn off the heat and use 2 forks to mix in the chopped tomato and garnish with coriander.

Re-cover the pan and leave to stand for 5 minutes.

To serve

Add a final pinch of garam masala powder and serve with spiced basmati rice.

Chef's tip

When you can smell the aroma of the masala spices, you know they are roasted and ready!

JALEBI

SERVES 6

🍷 *Prosecco Spumante DOC Treviso la Jara (Sparkling) (Italy)*

Method

Mix the plain flour and yoghurt to make a smooth, thick batter. Ensure the batter is kept at room temperature (30°c) for 24 hours (allowing for fermentation).

Following this time, stir the mixture to ensure there is an even consistency.

Next make a small hole in the centre of the muslin cloth, which will hold the jalebi mixture as it is released into the hot oil to fry. Place the oil on a high heat, when it is ready pour some of the batter into the cloth and begin to create round spirally shapes in the oil.

Allow to fry until the jalebi becomes golden brown. Once you have made enough jalebi, set aside. Next dissolve the sugar in a pan in 1 glass of water for about 20 minutes on a high heat. After this time set aside for cooling and add the saffron.

Once the temperature has reduced, dip the fried golden jalebi in the sugar syrup and leaved immersed for 2 minutes, then remove and serve hot.

To serve

Assemble as in the picture.

Chef's tip

It is best to use a flat frying pan, you will also need a muslin cloth.

Ingredients

500g plain flour
50g yoghurt (for fermentation)
2 litres cooking oil
2kg sugar
2 pinches saffron

090
THE DUKE OF WELLINGTON INN

Newton, Northumberland NE43 7UL

01661 844 446
www.thedukeofwellingtoninn.co.uk

The Duke of Wellington Inn is nestled in the Tyne valleys village of Newton, near Corbridge, within easy access to Newcastle, Hadrian's Wall Country, Hexham, and Northumberland's National Park. The Inn has recently reopened following an extensive refurbishment. The new décor reflects the traditional country inn history but with a modern twist. Existing oak and stone has been enhanced with modern colours, furniture and fabrics.

Lunches and dinners are served seven days a week in the bar and dining room. The food provides traditional British comfort eating to an exceptional standard and makes use of local, seasonal ingredients. Having seen our Executive Head Chef John Calton cook his way into the final of MasterChef the Professionals, the skill of John and his team offers a fine dining experience at the Inn allowing locals and visitors alike to sample luxury culinary skills. Our team make use of local in-season produce and ingredients, and with our menu refreshed on a daily basis, dining will always be a first class experience. A comprehensive range of beers and ales complements an extensive wine list.

The Inn experience continues with seven bedrooms providing a very high quality of luxury accommodation and a Northumbrian feel. There is a large variety of walking and cycling in the Tynedale area and a number of outstanding golf courses for those visitors who favour a less relaxing country break.

The outstanding views across the Tyne valley provide the ultimate conclusion to a visit to the Duke of Wellington which will stay with you long after you leave.

The Inn has recently reopened following an extensive refurbishment. The new décor reflects the traditional country inn history but with a modern twist. Existing oak and stone has been enhanced with modern colours, furniture and fabrics

PURPLE SPROUTING BROCCOLI WITH HOT MAYONNAISE AND BLOOD ORANGE

SERVES 4

Pinot Gris A.C.
Alsace Schoepfer (France) 2006

Method

For the main dish

Criss-cross the tomato skins with a sharp knife. Blanch in boiling water for 20 seconds and then plunge into iced water. Peel, wash, and deseed the tomatoes and dry out in an oven at 100°C for 5 hours.

Pick out the basil tip leaves and drop into boiling water for 5-10 seconds. Refresh in ice water, drain and blend with enough olive oil to make a puree.

Segment the blood oranges, keeping the centres to squeeze out the juice. Reduce the blood orange juice to syrup and chill. Double the volume of blood orange syrup with olive oil, whisking all the time until it emulsifies.

For the hot mayonnaise

Put the eggs, mustard, sherry vinegar and salt into a food processor. Whisk while adding the oils in a steady stream. When the oil is incorporated place the mixture into a cream whipper and add gas. Place the cream whipper into a pan of gently simmering water and shake every 2 minutes until the eggs have cooked out and the mayonnaise has a whipped egg white consistency.

To serve

Assemble as in the picture.

Ingredients

Main Dish

6 purple sprouting broccoli strands
2 plum tomatoes
1 bunch basil
1 bunch coriander
8 blood oranges
olive oil

Hot Mayonnaise

3 egg yolks
3 whole eggs
14g Maldon salt
14ml sherry vinegar
14g Dijon mustard
100ml olive oil
400ml vegetable oil

GOOSNARGH CORN FED DUCK WITH POTATO GNOCCHI, CARROTS AND RED WINE

SERVES 4

 Pinot Noir Vidal, Hawkes Bay (New Zealand) 2009

Ingredients

Carrots and Beetroot

200ml white wine vinegar
1 bottle white wine
20 coriander seeds
4 lemons (sliced)
200g sugar
1 raw beetroot (thinly sliced)
1 black carrot (thinly sliced)
1 red carrot (thinly sliced)

Gnocchi

5 medium red skin potatoes
3 egg yolks
100g flour
chives

Carrot Purée

6 carrots
100ml carrot juice
1 sprig thyme
2 cloves garlic
200g butter

Duck Sauce

500ml veal stock
500ml duck stock
10 button mushrooms
6 shallots
1 bottle red wine

Main Dish

1 duck breast
1 baby gem
chervil

Method

For the carrots and beetroot

To make the pickling liquor put the white wine vinegar, white wine, coriander seeds, lemons and sugar in a pan and bring to the boil. Take the pan off the heat and allow to cool. Sieve the liquid and pour over the sliced carrots and beetroots, keeping them separate.

For the gnocchi

Place the potatoes in an oven at 180°C for about 1 hour until soft inside with a crispy skin. Scoop out the potato with a spoon leaving the skin behind. Pass the potato through a drum sieve then add the egg yolks, flour and chives. Wrap the potato mixture in clingfilm in a sausage shape and tie the ends. Poach in water until firm then refresh in ice. When chilled, slice and take off the cling ilm ready to fry later.

For the carrot purée

Slice the carrots and sweat in butter with garlic and thyme. When softened add the carrot juice, bring to the boil and purée in a blender.

For the duck sauce

Sweat the mushrooms and shallots with thyme and garlic. Add the red wine and reduce to syrup. Add the veal and duck stocks and reduce to sauce consistency.

For the duck

Place the duck breast in a cold dry pan skin side down. Put the pan on a medium heat and cook till the skin is golden and crispy. Turn the duck breast over and fry for a further 3 minutes. Take the pan off the heat and allow the duck breast to carry on cooking in the pan for a further 10 minutes. Return the pan to the heat, add a small knob of butter and add the gnocchi. Fry gently until browned then add the baby gem until wilted.

To serve

Assemble in the picture using the chervil as a garnish.

RHUBARB CHEESECAKE WITH PISTACHIOS AND FENNEL GLASS

SERVES 4

Riesling Tardia, Vendimia (Chile) 2008

Ingredients

Cheesecake

300g Philadelphia cheese
300ml double cream
45g icing sugar
8 egg yolks
50g sugar
3 leaves of gelatine

Base

20 digestive biscuits
50g butter
squirt of honey

Rhubarb

Splash of red wine vinegar
1 tbsp sugar
4 forced rhubarb stalks

Jelly

4 pieces of forced rhubarb
100ml sugar
200ml water
2 leaves of gelatine

Garnish

A small handful of pistachio nuts (crushed)
4 Rhubarb and Custard boiled sweets (optional)
200g isomalt
fennel pollen

Method

For the cheesecake cream

Combine the icing sugar and cheese. Half whip the cream. Mix the sugar and water and combine to a soft ball, combine the egg yolks, whisking all the time. Re-hydrate the gelatine, drain and melt in the microwave. Add the gelatine to the egg and sugar mix. Combine all ingredients, mixed together and chill.

For the base

Blitz the biscuits in a food processor. Melt the honey and butter together and add to the biscuits.

For the rhubarb

Using a water bath - set the water bath temperature to 61°C. Put the rhubarb, vinegar and sugar in a vac bag. Line up the pieces of rhubarb in the bag and drop into the water bath. Cook until tender, this should take about 10 minutes. Refresh in ice.

Put the rhubarb, vinegar and sugar in a pan. Cover with water and until tender. Refresh in ice.

Keep the poaching juices for use later.

For the jelly

Cut the rhubarb into pieces and poach in a pan with the sugar and water until tender. Stir in re-hydrated gelatine and chill.

For the garnish

Heat the isomalt in a pan. When melted sprinkle in the fennel pollen and spread onto a sheet of baking paper. Chill until hard and snap into large shards.

Blitz the Rhubarb and Custard sweets to a coarse powder.

To serve

Assemble as in the picture.

FINBARR'S RESTAURANT

Waddington Street, Flass Vale, Durham City, DH1 4BG

0191 370 9999
www.finbarrsrestaurant.co.uk

Finbarr's Restaurant opened in February 2010. It is conveniently located within strolling distance of the centre of the beautiful, historic, City of Durham. After a complete refurbishment programme to set up the restaurant, the chic, contemporary décor provides guests with comfort and style as they enjoy their dining experience. In addition, a pleasant bar provides a relaxing space for pre or post dinner drinks.

Finbarr's was established as a partnership between Barry O'Leary, previously at the Cherry Tree, Jesmond, and Head Chef Tom Jackson, previously at Bistro 21.

Tom, a local lad, has built his reputation in the North East and is well known and respected throughout the region. His varied á la carte and table d'hote menus offer a mix of traditional, rustic and contemporary dining.

To complement this is a wine list characterised by the breadth and depth of the offering. Ranging from an Italian Prosecco Riserva 2008, to the Hawkes Bay Sauvignon Blanc 2008, not to mention the renowned Chateau Musar 2002 from the Lebanon. Food, service and a warm welcome are at the heart of what Finbarr's stands for.

After a complete refurbishment programme to set up the restaurant, the chic, contemporary décor provides guests with comfort and style as they enjoy their dining experience

HAGGIS SCOTCH EGG

SERVES 4

🍷 Coopers Creek Pinot Noir
Marlborough, New Zealand

Ingredients

Eggs

4 fresh hen eggs
200g good quality haggis
2 egg yolks
200g Panko breadcrumbs
3 whole eggs
dash of milk
100g flour

Purée

250g Boudin Noir
75ml boiling double cream
salt and pepper

Pancakes

115g of cold mashed potato
35g plain flour
2 tbsp softened butter

Garnish

Parsley and cooked bacon

Method

For the eggs

Bring pan of water, including a dash of white wine vinegar, to the boil.

Add the 4 fresh hen eggs, making sure they are at room temperature, and boil for exactly 7 minutes.

Plunge the cooked eggs into a bowl of icy water and leave for 5 minutes to cool.

Remove shells and place in the fridge.

Blend the haggis in a food processor with the 2 egg yolks and pulse until smooth.

Spread out the clingfilm on a smooth surface. Roll haggis mix between 2 sheets of clingfilm to ½ cm thick and chill.

Cut to 8cm squares and remove one side of the clingfilm. Wrap haggis mix around one of the cooked eggs, moulding the haggis around the egg. Rewrap with clingfilm and refrigerate.

Using 3 whole eggs, with a dash of milk, make an eggwash to help the breadcrumbs adhere. Lightly dust haggis encased eggs with flour, then plunge into the eggwash and roll in breadcrumbs.

Place on a tray and refrigerate.

To cook, deep fry at 160°C for 4 ½ minutes until golden brown.

For the purée

Place Boudin Noir in a microwave-proof bowl and cover with clingfilm.

Microwave on full power for 2 to 3 minutes.

Remove clingfilm, take care of the steam generated during cooking. Cut lengthways, remove flesh and place in a blender, slowly adding the cream until mixture is smooth.

Set aside and keep warm. Season if necessary.

For the pancakes

Mix all ingredients in bowl to make a soft dough.

Roll out on a well floured surface and cut to required size. Cook in a lightly oiled frying pan, on a medium heat until golden on each side.

To serve

Assemble as per the photo, adding parsley and a slice of cooked bacon to garnish.

FILLET OF HALIBUT WITH A PEA AND BACON FRICASEE

SERVES 4

Rias Baxias Albarino, Casel Caeiro
Spain

Ingredients

4 x 150g halibut portions
300g fresh peas (shelled)
70g shredded runner beans
50g shelled broad beans
200ml double cream
100g bacon/pancetta lardons
200ml fish stock
handful of parsley (chopped)
50g silver skin onions
20 mint leaves
150g cold butter (diced)
1 lemon

Method

Bring a medium sized pan of salted water to the boil. Add the peas and mint and simmer for one minute. Then strain through a colander.

Set 50g of cooked peas to one side.

Place the remaining peas and mint in a food blender and slowly add 100ml of boiling double cream until a smooth paste is achieved. Set aside and keep warm.

In a saucepan, reduce the fish stock to a syrup and add the remaining cream.

Bring to the boil and then whisk in the diced butter until all has been added. Keep warm.

For the halibut

Heat 2 tablespoons of olive oil in a large frying pan and season the halibut. Add the fish to the pan and fry for 4-5 minutes on a medium heat,. Turn once, and allow 4-5 minutes on the other side. Add a knob of butter and a squeeze of lemon juice. Baste the fish with the butter.

Add the remaining peas, broad beans, shredded runner beans, bacon and onions to the sauce. Finish with a squeeze of lemon juice and chopped parsley.

To assemble

Put a sizeable round of the pea purée in the middle of the plate. Add the halibut on top and finish with a spoonful of the pea sauce over the fish.

To serve

Serve with boiled or crushed new potatoes.

FRENCH APPLE TART

SERVES 4

🍷 *Pineau Des Charentes 10 yrs old Rouge by the house of Beaulon , France*

Ingredients

3/4 apples (peeled, cored and cut into slices just
before required)

Pastry

175g all purpose flour
85g soft unsalted butter
3 egg yolks
85g caster sugar
½ organic lemon (zest)
3 to 4 drops of vanilla extract
pinch of salt

Frangipane

175g ground almonds
175g soft unsalted butter
125g caster sugar
3 eggs
1 ½ tbsp of all purpose flour
1 tbsp Calvados or Kirsch
2 drops of almond extract

Glaze

apricot jam
lemon juice

Method

For the pastry

Sift the flour into a food processor. Add all other pastry
ingredients. Mix until pastry forms a ball. Do not overwork or the
pastry will become tough.

Wrap and place in refrigerator for 1 hour.

Roll out and put into a greased flan dish. Return to refrigerator
for 30 minutes.

Bake blind for 7 - 8 minutes (place greaseproof paper over the
pastry and fill with beans or baking beans).

Remove the baking beans and paper and bake for another 5-7
minutes, until light golden brown.

For the frangipane

Mix the butter and sugar until creamy. Add the eggs, ground
almonds, sifted flour, Calvados and almond extract and mix.

Fill the pastry case with the frangipane, not quite to the top.

Place the sliced apples evenly on top, bake at 200°C for 30 - 40
minutes.

For the glaze

Heat the jam gently until it melts, add the lemon juice and mix
in, push through a sieve.

When cool, remove from baking dish and brush the glaze over
the top.

To serve

Serve with vanilla ice cream.

110
GREENHOUSE BRASSERIE

Quarryfield Road, Gateshead College, Gateshead NE8 3BE

0191 490 2414
www.greenhousebrasserie.com

Established in 2009, the Greenhouse Brasserie is a commercial restaurant within Gateshead College. We chose the name to emphasise our ethos to grow and train young talent for the hospitality industry.

We pride ourselves in offering great customer service with that personal touch. Our chef Graham Johns has created a menu emphasising natural, honest cooking with simple, elegant, 'Modern British Cuisine', sourcing his ingredients from renowned local producers. Graham brings over 20 years of experience, having joined Greenhouse Brasserie following his work at The Arch in Tynemouth, Linden Hall and Beamish Hall.

We encourage a collective approach, valuing contributions and critique from customers, waiters and chefs alike. This collaboration, along with good sourcing, seasonal changes to dishes and encouraging spontaneity, all help to keep the menu alive.

Apart from the delicious food served in our restaurant, we also offer a bespoke event service, catering for private and business events throughout our region. The events part of our business has been as successful as the restaurant; we are growing, with satisfied customers every week. Our events menu can be accessed via our web site.

Food and service is our passion. We like our guests to relax in our comfortable contemporary restaurant and indulge in our seasonal menus with a good selection of wines.

greenhouse SPECIALS

Petit Greek Salad
Soup of the day
Chicken Truffle Terrine
£

Pan Fried Sea Bream
almond & parsley crust, pea & mint Risotto
French Steak, Dauphinoise Potato
vegetables, red wine jus
Seared Monkfish
and 3 spring onion mash, pinta
Chops, champ, Baby Vegetables

..... Risotto
..... Honey Purée

..... course £10

greenhouse
BRASSERIE

greenhouse

Special winter promotion

Baileys liqueur coffee
Usual price £6.00 – our promotion price £3.00 each.

Why not try this lovely winter warmer with a cookie or
cake or as a delicious after
dinner drink.

Food and service is our passion. We like our guests to relax in our comfortable contemporary restaurant and indulge in our seasonal menus with a good selection of wines

NORTHUMBRIAN WOOD PIGEON, ON A CELERIAC AND POTATO ROSTI, SPRING SALAD LEAVES AND RED WINE JUS

SERVES 1

🍷 *Cabernet Sauvignon Merlot, Central Valley, Siete Soles, CHILE*

Ingredients

1 x 60g pigeon breast
100g of celeriac (peeled and grated)
½ a potato (peeled and grated)
1 shallot (finely diced)
1 egg yolk
butter

Method

For the rosti

Place the celeriac, potato, shallot and egg yolk into a medium size bowl.

Grease a tray and place the mixture into it, to a depth of around 1 inch.

Place in a preheated oven at 150°C, and cook until the celeriac and potato is tender (15-20mins but keep checking).

Once cooked, remove from the oven and place on a cooling rack to cool.

When cool, get a circle cutter and cut, approximately 2-3 medium size rostis.

For the pigeon breast

Place a pan on a high heat and let it warm up.

Oil and season the pigeon breast and place into a smoking hot pan laying it away from your body to avoid any splash-back of hot oil.

Cook for 1 minute on either side, then add a knob of butter and place in the oven at 180°C for a further minute. Remove and rest.

Pigeon is best served medium rare. Add or subtract time to your preference.

To serve

Serve with spring leaves and red wine jus as seen in the picture.

Chef's tip

Pigeon cooks very quickly and is easy to over cook.

MONKFISH AND FRUITS OF THE SEA BALLOTINE SERVED WITH SPRING VEGETABLES

SERVES 1

🍷 Sauvignon Blanc
Central Valley, CHILE

Ingredients

185g monkfish
60g smoked salmon
150g rainbow trout fillet
1 beef tomato
300g potato purée
1 tbsp parsley (chopped)
pinch of salt and pepper
200g unsalted butter
150ml olive oil
150ml apple juice
2 drops lemon flavouring
1 tsp of Agar Agar

Method

For the monkfish

Fillet the monkfish and clean off all of the membrain.

Season with salt and pepper and wrap tightly with clingfilm.

Poach for 12 minutes then refresh in iced water.

Make a purée out of the trout fillet, wrap in clingfilm and set aside in the fridge.

Concasse (roughly chop) the tomato and finely dice the black olive. Add the chopped parsley and season, then add to the potato purée.

To assemble

Unwrap the monkfish, pat it dry and coat it in smoked salmon. Then add the trout purée and gently pan fry it in olive oil and butter until golden brown.

To serve

Cut through the monkfish diagonally and present on the plate. Then whisk up the apple juice, lemon flavouring and agar agar until its foams up. Then pour over the fish.

SUMMER BEE

SERVES 10-12

🍷 *Prosecco Brut,*
Argeo - Ruggeri NV

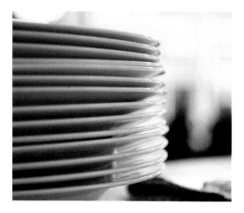

Ingredients

Honeycomb Tuille

75g clear honey
140g liquid glucose
400g sugar
5 tbsp water
2 tbsp baking soda

English Rose and Honey Ice Cream

12 egg yolks (large free range eggs if possible)
30g of caster sugar
25g of liquid glucose
100ml of whole milk
150ml of double cream
1 tbsp of honey
2 tbsp of English rose compound
1 tbsp of ice cream stabilizer

Method

For the honeycomb tuille

Line a shallow baking tray with parchment paper.

Place the honey, liquid glucose, water and sugar in a large heavy-based saucepan and heat gently, stirring occasionally until the sugar dissolves.

Increase the heat and cook until the mixture starts to turn a light golden colour.

Mix in the baking soda and whisk the mixture quickly. Pour immediately into the prepared baking tray.

Allow to cool. Once cool place in a airtight container.

Blitz the honeycomb and sieve the powdered honeycomb over a stencil or shape you desire.

Place in the oven at 200°C for approximately 40 seconds to melt it together and with a pallet knife, carefully slide off the baking parchment onto a cold surface to harden.

This recipe will make at least 20 tuilles.

For the english rose and honey ice cream

Place the milk, cream, glucose and honey, over a medium heat, in a heavy bottomed pan. Do not boil.

Place the egg yolks and sugar in a bowl and whisk over a bain-marie until pale in colour. This is called a sabayon.

When you can see the beginning of steam from the cream and milk pour one third into the sabayon. Once mixed thoroughly add the remainder and return to the heat.

Heat for a further 5 minutes, keeping the temperature below 65°C.

Once the crème anglais coats the back of a spoon, bring off the heat and add the English rose compound and stabilizer. Strain the anglais, place into tubs and store in the freezer until needed (Please note we use a paco jet, which is specialised equipment however this recipe usually is soft enough without the use of one).

To serve

Assemble as in the picture.

Chef's tips

Please note do not allow moisture to get to the honeycomb, any moisture will make the honeycomb unworkable.

Dip your finger into the crème anglais, if it's too hot to stand then bring it off the heat.

120
HEADLAM HALL

Headlam, Nr Gainford, Darlington DL2 3HA

01325 730 238
www.headlamhall.co.uk

This Jacobean manor house stands in beautiful walled gardens, surrounded by its own rolling farmland in the picturesque countryside of lower Teesdale. Voted North East Small Hotel of the Year 2009/10, this independent family owned hotel offers forty individually designed bedrooms, a luxury spa, a challenging golf course and an award winning restaurant. Under the guidance of Head Chef, David Hunter, the restaurant serves imaginative dishes using the best of locally sourced ingredients, including produce from the Hall's own gardens and farm.

Strong relationships with local suppliers are at the core of this philosophy and a good example is local farmer and butcher, Joe Simpson, who has been working closely with Headlam for over 25 years.

The restaurant at Headlam Hall is set in the elegant Orangery with its tranquil colours, and the intimate Panel Room with its warm ambiance. There are excellent private dining facilities with three rooms including the delightful Georgian Drawing Room that overlooks the terrace and main lawn. Larger events, including wedding receptions can be catered for in the Edwardian Suite characterised by an arched glass ceiling and oak flooring. Whether it is a meal for two or one hundred the same high standards of catering apply combined with friendly and courteous service.

Under the guidance of Head Chef, David Hunter, the restaurant serves imaginative dishes using the best of locally sourced ingredients including produce from the Hall's own gardens and farm

COTHERSTONE CHEESE PARFAIT WITH RED WINE POACHED PEAR, GINGER BREAD, TOASTED HAZELNUTS AND A RED WINE SYRUP

SERVES 4

🍷 *Gewurztraminer, Joseph Cattin, Alsace, France*

Ingredients

Parfait

200g Cotherstone cheese crumbled
2tbsps crème fraiche
½ tsp lemon juice
1tsp honey
salt and pepper

Gingerbread

50g caster sugar
240g strong white flour
20g baking powder
2tsp mixed spice
2tsp ground ginger
zest of 1 lemon and 1 orange
250g clear honey
3 eggs
2 tsp vanilla extract

Pears

2 pears (peeled and cored, cut into quarters)
½ bottle red wine
2 star anise
100g caster sugar
75ml blackcurrant cordial

Method

For the parfait

Blitz everything in a food processer until smooth add a touch of water if too thick, pass through a sieve and chill.

For the pears

Put all ingredients in a pan and simmer until soft, leave pears to cool in liquid, when cool remove pears and reduce cooking liquid to syrup and chill

For the gingerbread

Grease a 4" by 8" loaf tin and preheat oven to 150°C.

Mix all dry ingredients together. Beat all wet ingredients together and then combine to make a batter, pour into loaf tin and cook for 35 minutes or until a skewer comes out clean.

To serve

Quenelle parfait and top with fanned slices of pear. Cut ginger bread, lightly toast it and place on side. Drizzle with red wine syrup, toasted hazelnuts and some rocket leaves.

RARE ROASTED FILLET OF 28 DAY AGED BEEF WITH BRAISED OX CHEEK, SPICED CARROT PURÉE, SPRING CABBAGE, PICKLED BABY ONIONS AND A THYME SCENTED JUS

SERVES 4

 Malbec, Kaiken, Argentina

Ingredients

1 whole beef fillet trimmed and wrapped tight in cling film

Ox cheek

2 ox cheeks
2 carrots, 2 onions, 2 sticks of celery and 2 sprigs of thyme (roughly diced)
enough beef stock to cover
salt and pepper

Pickled Baby Onions

20 baby onions (peeled and blanched for 1 minute)
200ml white wine vinegar
45g caster sugar
2 cardamon pods and cloves
1 cinnamon stick and 1 star anise

Carrot purée

3 carrots diced
½ star anise
120g butter
100ml chicken stock

Thyme jus

500ml cooking liquid (from the ox cheeks)
sprig of thyme
knob of butter

Garnish

spring cabbage
crisp pancetta
roast potato

Method

For the fillet

Unwrap the fillet then season and seal on all sides in a very hot pan. Cook at 180°C for 9 mins and leave to rest in a warm place.

For the ox cheek

Season and seal the ox cheek and add vegetables and stock. Cook in a moderate oven for 2hrs or until soft. When cool enough to handle, flake meat into a bowl adjust seasoning and wrap tightly in clingfilm making a thick cigar shape. Chill.

For the pickled baby onions

Place all ingredients in a pan apart from the onions and bring to the boil. Peel onions and trim the ends, pour over the boiling vinegar mixture and leave to chill. These are best made at least a day in advance.

For the carrot purée

Place all ingredients in a pan. Cook slowly until soft then take out the star anise and strain off the liquid.

Blitz in a food processor, adding back a little of the cooking liquid until completely smooth, pass through a sieve and keep warm.

For the thyme jus

Bring cooking liquid to the boil with the thyme then reduce by half and whisk in the butter. Pass and correct the seasoning.

To serve

Place a spoonful of carrot purée to the plate and drag a spoon through it, place the spring cabbage in the centre then add a couple of roast potatoes, slice the ox cheek and pan fry until heated through and add to the plate,.

Warm the pickled onions and place 3 around each plate, carve the fillet and place on top of the cabbage.

Then spoon on some sauce and finally top with a slice of crispy bacon.

HEADLAM HALL BANOFFEE PIE WITH BANANA ICE-CREAM, CARAMELISED BANANA SPONGE AND BANANA PRALINE

SERVES 4

🍷 *Chateau La Fleur D'Or,*
Sâuternes 2006

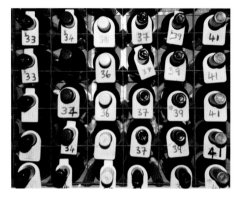

Ingredients

Base

6 digestive biscuits (crushed)
50g butter

Ganache

140g dark chocolate
100ml cream
7g butter

Caramel Mousse

½ tin condensed milk boiled for 2 ½ hours and
left to go cold
200ml double cream
1 leaf gelatine

Caramelised Banana

1 banana

Vanilla Cream

100ml cream
¼ vanilla pod seeds
20g sugar

Method

For the banoffee pie

Begin by making the base. Melt the butter, mix it into the crushed biscuits and press into 4 moulds.

For the ganache

Simmer cream, butter and chocolate until melted.

Whisk until cool and place in a piping bag.

For the caramel mousse

Whisk condensed milk until smooth. Dissolve gelatine in a little cream then add to caramel with the rest of cream and whisk until firm. Place into a piping bag.

For the caramelised banana

Thinly slice one banana, dust with icing sugar and caramelise with a blow torch.

For the vanilla cream

Whip cream sugar, and vanilla together until it forms stiff peaks place into a piping bag.

To serve

Pipe a layer of chocolate ganache into the moulds on top of the biscuit base and chill until firm.

Next pipe a layer of caramel mousse and chill until firm.

Then add the caramelised banana.

Finally pipe on the vanilla cream and grate over some chocolate.

Chef's tip

We serve the banoffee pie with banana ice-cream, caramelised banana cake, salted caramel and banana tuile as seen in the picture.

130
HOTEL DU VIN & BISTRO

City Road, Newcastle Upon Tyne NE1 2BE

0191 229 2200
www.hotelduvin.com

Hotel du Vin Newcastle is set on the banks of the River Tyne and commands outstanding views of Newcastle Quayside and the bridges. This former home of the Tyne Tees Steam Shipping Company has been gloriously converted into 42 luxurious bedrooms, trademark bistro, an intriguing Laroche tasting room, two stunning private dining rooms, Bubble bar, a courtyard for alfresco dining and an outstanding wine cellar. Open seven days a week, and under the tutelage of head chef, Ross Bootland, the bistro is at the heart of our hotel. A classic, French styled, elegant and informal setting for lunch, dinner, to meet, celebrate or simply pass the time. Dine in the finest produce that Northumberland has to offer from our local heroes such, as seasonal vegetables and Heritage Potatoes from Tiptoe Farm, eggs from Sunny Hill and kippers from The Craster Smoke House. These are only a handful of the many legendary suppliers we are honoured to share our Homegrown and Local philosophy with. Add to this our extensive and eclectic wine list. Wine is the reason why we're here. Without it there is no du Vin, but we never want you to be mystified by the jargon and mumbo-jumbo that often surrounds the appreciation of wine. Let our Sommelier Ian Cobham guide you through our wine list showcasing the great wines available in the world today.

For those that wish to make a night of it the 42 timelessly styled bedrooms and stunning suites, all featuring luxurious handsprung mattresses, fine Egyptian linen, deep baths and powerful drench showers, plasma TVs, DVDs and air conditioning.

Open seven days a week, and under the tutelage of head chef, Ross Bootland, the bistro is at the heart of our hotel. A classic, French styled, elegant and informal setting for lunch, dinner, to meet, celebrate or simply pass the time

ROASTED BEETROOT WITH GOAT'S CHEESE SALAD

SERVES 4

🍷 *Sancerre Terres Blanches, Domaine Thomas & Fils, Loire Centre 2009*

Ingredients

1 kg of red beetroot
2 cloves of garlic
1 sprig of thyme
10g of maldon sea salt
1 sprig of rosemary
10ml extra virgin olive oil
mesclun salad leaves mix

Honey Dressing

50ml extra virgin olive oil
2 tbsp of clear honey
1 tsp Dijon mustard

Method

Wash the beetroot put in a heavy based pan then cover with water from the tap.

Chop the garlic, thyme and rosemary and place in the same pan.

Bring to boil and simmer for 10 minutes.

Drain the water and peel the beetroot. (Be careful it will be hot so you might want to put some rubber gloves on).

Once peeled, square off and dice up to 1cm cubes. Place in a warm pan and roast off in 10ml of extra virgin olive oil. Add a dash of balsamic vinegar with salt and pepper to taste.

Roughly arrange in the centre of the plate, then arrange the goats cheese on top and place under the grill or in the oven for a couple of minutes.

For the honey dressing

Put mustard and honey in a bowl, whisk in the olive oil and season to taste.

To serve

Roughly arrange the mesclun lettuce leaves on top of the beetroot and goat's cheese and finish by drizzling over the honey dressing.

SMOKED HADDOCK FISH CAKE

SERVES 4

 Encruzado, Casa de Santar
Dao 2008

Ingredients

Fish Cakes

500g smoked haddock
400ml milk
300g mashed potatoes (dry)
1 bunch spring onions
1 sheet butter paper

Butter Sauce

1 shallot
100ml white wine
10ml white wine vinegar
1 sprig thyme
10ml cream

200g spinach
4 eggs
1 packet butter (diced)
1 bunch chives (chopped)

Method

For the fishcakes

Poach the smoked haddock in milk making sure that your fish flakes are still translucent, then wash and slice your spring onions.

Mix together the smoked haddock, mash, spring onions and then season.

Weigh out 200g portions, mould into round shapes and set aside.

For the sauce

Peel and slice the shallot and place into a pan with the white wine, white wine vinegar and thyme. Reduce liquid down until there is no liquid left. Add the cream and then slowly add the butter. Pass through a chinois and set aside somewhere warm.

Pan-fry the fish cake for 45 seconds on each side and finish off in the oven on a sheet of butter paper for 5 minutes, check the fish cake is warm enough when it comes out.

For the spinach and poached eggs

Sweat off the spinach in a frying pan with a little oil and season. Poach the eggs and warm up the butter sauce adding the chopped chives.

To serve

Assemble as in the picture.

CUSTARD TART

SERVES 8

🍷 *Beerenauslese HdV Label, Willi Opitz, Austria 2006*

Ingredients

Filling

270g egg yolks
150g caster sugar
1litre double cream

Sweet Pastry

500g plain flour
250g soft butter
180g caster sugar
2 eggs
2 vanilla pods seeds only
pinch of salt

whole nutmeg

Method

For the pastry

Cream butter, sugar and vanilla seeds.

Mix in the eggs, then sift in the flour and salt.

Mix until it clumps then knead in the dough with your hands.

Wrap in clingfilm and rest in the fridge for at least an hour.

Roll out the pastry and line a prepared loose bottom tart tin.

Chill, then fill with clingfilm and baking beans.

Blind bake for 20 minutes at 160°C, remove the beans and bake for a further 10 minutes.

Egg wash and bake for a further 2 minutes.

Cool tart case.

For the filling

Whisk together the egg yolks and sugar until pale then add the cream.

Heat the mixture to 37°C then pass and chill.

Rest overnight.

Place tart case on a tray in the oven on 120°C.

Pour in the filling as high as you can, bake for 1 hour 15 minutes or until the tart is set, with a pot of water on the bottom shelf to create some steam.

Remove the tart from the oven and grate a whole nutmeg on top of it.

Leave to cool before chilling in the fridge and portioning.

To serve

Assemble as in the picture.

140
MALMAISON NEWCASTLE

Quayside, Newcastle upon Tyne NE1 3DX

0191 245 5000
www.malmaison.com

A bridge that winks. Now there's a thing. Then you get it, sitting in the bar looking out over the river Tyne. A winking bridge needs something utterly gorgeous to wink at. Your chosen room for tonight is on the seventh. An entire floor of suites dedicated to the glory of shipbuilding. Meanwhile, deep in the basement a seductive day spa lies in wait.

The Malmaison brasserie is the perfect place to enjoy a stylish supper. Relax and soak up the atmosphere in intimate booths and restore your spirits with a delicious and sophisticated menu made from the finest local ingredients.

Three unique private dining rooms are popular for client functions and private parties. Nicely intimate, the 10, 12 and 30 capacity rooms offer parties the opportunity to dine in private and opulent or quirky (depending on your choice of room) surroundings while still enjoying the ambience of a busy brasserie with top class food and service.

Simple classic dishes, uncompromising in quality and generous in portions. "I'm having a love affair with the local food heroes of Northumberland" you think as you browse the menu. Every ingredient comes from around the corner, genuinely prepared with passion by head chef Drew Heron and his team of superstar chefs. Northumberland steak and ale pie it is.

Eating out in Newcastle has never been so good at the Mal. The 80 seater Brasserie is decadent, rich in colour and design. Enter through the candle lit stairway for the ultimate dining experience, complemented with the finest wines carefully selected by our expert Sommelier.

Drew and his team of chefs and waiters have worked hard to develop a truly unique dining experience in Newcastle which keeps the restaurant busy seven nights a week.

Simple classic dishes, uncompromising in quality and generous in portions. "I'm having a love affair with the local food heroes of Northumberland" you think as you browse the menu

HAM HOCK ROULADE, PEASE PUDDING AND STOTTIE BREAD

SERVES 4

🍷 *Andante, Gewürztraminer/Muscat, Cave de Ribeauvillé, Alsace, France, 2009*

Ingredients

1 good size ham hock
2 prosciutto (sliced)
5g parsley (chopped)
4 portions of micro cress

Pease Pudding

75g yellow split peas
500ml ham stock (from ham hock)
½ carrot (chopped)
4 portions of stottie bread

Method

For ham hock

Wash off the ham hock in cold running water for half an hour so that the ham is not too salty. Place into a suitable pot, bring to the boil and simmer for 3-4 hours until the ham is falling off the bone, then allow to cool down in the ham stock. Lift the ham from the stock and pick the meat from the bone, discarding the fat. Keep the ham stock to one side.

Once the ham is picked, place into a bowl add in the chopped parsley and season with a little pepper. Take a large clingfilm 22"and roll it out towards you. Place 4-5 proscuitto slices just overlapping each other onto the clingfilm. Carefully place the moist but not wet ham hock mix along the proscuitto slices enough that you will end up with a 1.5" cylinder shape once rolled tight but not too much mix as this will hinder the rolling. Once happy that you have enough filling roll the proscuitto around the ham hock mix. Once rolled tie the ends of the clingfilm to ensure the mix will not come out of the ends of the roulade. Get a friend to hold the clingfilm tight and you start to roll it away from you making sure you apply pressure to the roulade as you roll it away from you. Once rolled leave in the fridge until the roulade becomes firm, slice a portion and ensure that all the clingfilm is removed.

For the pease pudding

Bring the yellow split peas to the boil with cold water. Once brought to the boil drain water. Add in the ham stock (approx 200ml) and chopped carrot to the peas, bring to the boil and simmer until cooked through. Do not season yet.

Add the warm ham stock to the peas as you go (until it reaches a medium consistency). When cold check the seasoning. When it cools you should be able to quenelle the pease pudding.

For the stottie bread

Halve the bread and cut into triangles, toast just before serving.

For micro cress

Snip the cress into a bowl of cold water, drain then dry on a cloth. Keep in an air tight container.

To serve

Slice the roulade into 4 good sized portions and place onto a clean, cold plate. To the right, place a quenelle of pease pudding and to the front of this place the toasted stottie bread. Garnish with a little micro cress and serve at once.

Chef's tip

The clingfilm will help you roll it out just as if you are making a roll up cigarette think of the proscuitto as the paper and the ham hock filling as the tobacco.

ROAST COLEY, VEGETABLE CAPONATA, MAIZE BUTTER SAUCE

SERVES 4

🍷 *Friendly Grüner Veltliner, Laurenz V, Kamptal, Austria, 2009*

Ingredients

4 x165g Coley fillet (skin on)

Maize stock

2 whole corn cobs

Caponata

15ml olive oil
2g garlic purée
15g baby capers
1 small peppers (diced)
1 small green courgette (diced)
½ small aubergine skin (diced)
1 small celery (diced)
1 shallot (finely diced)
50ml reduced tomato juice

8 small black olives (diced)
2 small anchovy fillets (diced)
5g parsley (finely chopped)

Maize Butter Sauce

maize stock
25ml double cream
70g cold butter (diced)

Method

For the maize stock

De-husk the corn (remove the outer leaves), cut into slices and cover with water and reduce by 90%. Then eat or discard the corn. Chill the maize stock.

For the caponata

Have ready all the caponata ingredients. Using a little olive oil, sauté off the peppers for 2 minutes then add the celery and sauté for another minute.

Add the shallots and garlic for 1 minute then add the courgette and aubergine, sautéing for a further 2 minutes. Quickly add in the reduced tomato juice, check seasoning and quickly blast the chilli down.

For the coley fillet

Ensure the coley fillet has been trimmed and is bone free,. Keep stored in the fridge on a cloth until ready.

For the maize butter sauce

Add a little of the cold maize stock to a small saucepan and bring to the boil. Add in a little of the double cream. Once this has reduced by ⅓, pull the pan to the side and monte (whisk) in the butter a bit at a time, not too fast and not too slow as this has to be kept 'warm'. If it gets too hot or too cold it will split (separate).

To assemble

Roast off the coley in a suitable non stick pan and cook in the oven at 180°C for approx 8 minutes until almost cooked through (if you have a probe take this to 72°C),. Keep warm.

In a suitable sized pan, warm through the vegetable caponata and add in the diced olives. As you pass it over add in the anchovy and chopped parsley.

To serve

In the centre of a plate place a portion of the caponata. Flash the coley under a grill and carefully place onto the caponata. Pour a portion of the maize butter sauce around the fish and serve at once.

KEY LIME PIE

SERVES 4

🍷 *Muscat de Beaumes de Venise, Domaine de Fenouillet, Southern Rhône, France, 2009*

Ingredients

Tuile Mix

200g caster sugar
100g butter
210g egg whites
75g honey
200g plain flour (sieved)

Biscuit Base

95g butter
175g digestive biscuit
50g granola cereal

Filling

1 tbsp lime zest
75ml lime juice
2 egg yolks
200g condensed milk

Ice Cream

125ml milk
125ml double cream
65g sugar
3 egg yolk
125g mascarpone cheese

Garnish

lime syrup
whipped cream

Method

For the tuille mix

This mixture can be made in advance and kept in the fridge. The ingredients are better to mix at room temperature.

Cream the sugar and butter in a bowl, slowly add in the egg whites and honey. Carefully add in the flour and mix well. Chill down in the fridge until completely cold.

For the biscuit base

Crush the digestive biscuits and granola. Melt the butter in a suitable sized pan and add the crumb mix. Butter and silicon-line a gastronorm tray and carefully press in the biscuit mix. Bake this in the oven at 180°C for about 10-12 minutes until crisp and golden brown

For the filling

Place egg yolks and lime zest into the mixer and whisk for about 2 minutes until the eggs thicken. Add in the condensed milk and whisk for another 4-5 minutes. Then add in the lime juice and give it a quick whisk, pouring the mix onto the crumb base and bake in the oven at 160°C for approx 20 minutes or until cooked. Chill this down and portion out into square portions, cover in cling film and keep chilled.

For the ice cream

Whisk the sugar and yolks in a bowl until almost white. Boil the milk and cream in a thick based pan. Whisk onto the egg and sugar mix, mix in well. Return to a clean saucepan and place on a low heat. Stir continuously with a wooden spoon until the mixture coats the back of the spoon. Pass through a sieve into a clean bowl. Whisk in the mascarpone cheese. Churn in an ice cream machine. Keep frozen.

For the tuile basket

Have ready the tuile mix and spread into a round cut-out stencil, making sure this is not too thick and bake at 180°C for about 6 minutes. Quickly place onto a suitable sized mould and set the biscuit you have, keep the mat on the hot tray as you do each basket (if not the tuille biscuits will set before you get a chance to mould them into a basket shape). Keep in an air tight container.

To serve

On the top left of a plate place one portion of the key lime pie. Move around the plate and place a little whipped cream to hold the basket. Top this with the basket. Carefully scoop a round ball of the mascarpone ice cream into the basket. Spoon a little lime syrup around the plate and serve at once.

150
THE MORRITT

Greta Bridge, Nr Barnard Castle, Co. Durham DL12 9SE

01833 627 232
www.themorritt.co.uk

The Morritt Country House Hotel surprises and delights.

This centuries-old hotel in beautiful Teesdale in County Durham is renowned for its Gilroys restaurant - vibrant colours, a touch of black leather, comfortable armchairs, silk blinds over window seats, fun artwork and a great atmosphere.

There's always something interesting on the menu – try the intriguing parsnip ice cream - and Chef Lee Stainthorpe changes the line-up with the seasons, cleverly making classic ideas fit the time of year.

The Morritt's owners are Barbara Johnson and her husband Peter Phillips. They believe that you only get out what you put in - quality dishes are rarely produced without quality ingredients.

Barbara says, 'It's important to be innovative and to know what goes into our dishes. If we have confidence in the provenance and quality, so will our customers.'

Barbara and Peter try to source quality local suppliers, but they've gone a step further. A herb garden at the hotel and fruit from the plum trees go into chutneys for the meat and cheeseboards.

A vine at Barbara and Peters' home in Neasham near Darlington in County Durham provides grapes for the cheeseboard, and an orchard of mature Bramley apples contributes to pies and crumbles.

They have also moved into livestock with free range hens and a few English rare breed pigs – Iron Age and Oxford Sandy and Blacks - who relish the windfall apples.

There's always something interesting on the menu – try the intriguing parsnip ice cream – and Chef Lee Stainthorpe changes the line-up with the seasons, cleverly making classic ideas fit the time of year

PAN FRIED SEA BASS, BROWN SHRIMP RISOTTO, BEETROOT, CHORIZO, PEA SHOOTS

SERVES 4

President's Selection Chardonnay
(bin 5)

Method

For the sea bass

Trim and halve the sea bass fillets then cut the skin.

For the beetroot

Dice the beetroot into 1cm pieces. Put the trimmings in a pan with 150ml of water, simmer and purée.

Add the stock to the purée, then adding a little sugar, reduce until a syrup consistency is reached. Allow to cool.

For the chorizo

Cut the chorizo into small batons.

For the chevril

Pick and chop the chervil and place in a food processor.

Heat the oil to approximately 85°C. Pour the oil over the herbs and blitz. Pass the oil through a cloth and cool.

For the shrimp risotto

Cook the risotto. When ready add the shrimp to warm through, cover and keep warm.

To assemble

In a hot frying-pan, heat a little oil and butter. Season the fish and fry skin-side down, allow to colour slightly.

Turn and squeeze lemon over the fillet, remove pan from the heat when cooked through.

Clean the pan, add the chorizo and beetroot and warm through.

To serve

Assemble and finish the dish as shown using the pea shoots to garnish and dressing the plate with the chervil oil.

Ingredients

4 sea bass fillets
100g risotto rice
70g brown shrimp
1 shallot
400ml vegetable stock
50g chorizo
2 cooked beetroots
1 bunch chervil
150ml olive oil
½ a lemon
50g butter
pea shoots for garnish

GRESSINGHAM DUCK 3 WAYS, POMMES DAUPHINOUS, FINE BEANS, ROAST FIG AND PURÉE

SERVES 4

🍷 Anapai
(bin 140)

Ingredients

2 duck breasts
2 duck legs
1 chicken fillet
150ml cream
4 pasta sheets
1 carrot
1 stick of celery
1 shallot
300ml reduced beef stock
30g pistachios
30g dried apricots
2 litres duck fat
100g butter
100ml red wine
20 fine beans (5 per person)

Roast Fig Purée

8 figs

Pommes Dauphinous

4 baking potatoes
300ml cream
2 garlic cloves
100g gruyere

Method

For the duck part 1

Carefully remove the skin from the legs and put to one side.

Salt the legs overnight.

Rinse and pat dry. Place in a tray, cover with duck fat and foil the tray. Place in an oven at 110°C for 4 hours. Remove the legs and drain. Pick off the meat and flake.

For the vegetables

Finely dice the carrot, celery and shallot and blanch. Place 100ml of reduced beef stock in a pan and heat. Add the diced butter and whisk. Pour over half the leg meat and vegetable brunoise and cool.

Trim the beans and blanch for 30 seconds.

For the duck part 2

Add the chicken fillet to a food processor and blitz. When it's a paste, slowly add the cream until smooth, then season and add the remains of the leg, chopped pistachio and apricot. Place the mix in the leg skin and roll to a sausage shape. Wrap in clingfilm and poach gently, in seasoned water for 40 to 50 minutes.

For the ravioli

Cook the pasta sheets for 2 minutes in salted, boiling water until tender. Remove and plunge into cold water. When cool, remove, dry and cut in half.

Spoon a small amount of the confit leg and vegetable mix into the middle of 4 halves. Brush the edge with egg yolk. Place the remaining sheets on top and nip round the edges to seal.

Just before serving, put into simmering salted water for 1 minute to reheat.

For the roast fig purée

Peel and place 8 figs in a small pan with 100ml red wine. Simmer until cooked, then purée.

For the pommes dauphinous

Peel and slice the potatoes. Boil with cream and garlic and arrange in a tray. Bake for 80 minutes at 160°C until the potato is tender. Grate the cheese and sprinkle over the potato. Bake for a further 10 minutes until golden.

For the duck part 3

Trim and score the duck breast's skin. Add skin-side down to a cold pan heat up and roast for 10 to 12 minutes. Remove, pour off fat and add figs. Roast for 4 minutes.

To serve

Assemble and finish the dish as shown.

CHOCOLATE TERRINE, STRAWBERRY PARFAIT, VANILLA MASCARPONE, PISTACHIO DUST, PRALINE WAFER

SERVES 4

 Muscat de Beaumes de Venise

Ingredients

Chocolate Terrine

200g dark chocolate
1 large egg
30g icing sugar
250ml double cream

Vanilla Mascarpone

200g mascarpone
1 tbsp honey

Strawberry Parfait

400g strawberries
200ml cream
1 sachet of gelatine

Pistachio Dust

50g pistachio nuts

Praline Wafer

200g caster sugar
50g hazelnuts
1 vanilla pod

Method

For the chocolate terrine

Melt the chocolate over a bain-marie. Whip half the cream to soft peaks. Separate the egg, beat the yolk with the icing sugar and whisk to a full peak. Allow the chocolate to cook slightly, add the yolk mix then fold in the cream, followed by the whisked egg whites. Pour into prepared moulds and refrigerate for 4 hours.

For the vanilla mascarpone

Scrape the vanilla and mix into the mascarpone, sweeten with honey if desired.

For the strawberry parfait

In the other pan, add the strawberries and cook until soft. Puree and pass. Add half the gelatine whilst warm and dissolve.

Whip the remainder of the cream and fold into the strawberry puree. Pour into suitable moulds and freeze.

For the pistachio dust

Gently roast the pistachio. When cold, blitz in a food processor or coffee grinder and sieve.

For the praline wafer

Add half the sugar and 3 tbsp water to each of two pans. In the first pan, allow the mixture to boil then cook to caramel. Add the hazelnuts then pour onto a greased bench or silicone paper. Allow to cool.

When the caramel and hazelnuts are cold, blitz in a processor to a course powder, reshape on a baking mat of silicone tray, re-bake for 190°C for 3/4 minutes and cool.

To serve

Finish and assemble the dish as shown.

160
O DE V

Pipewellgate House, Pipewellgate, Gateshead Quayside, Tyne & Wear NE8 2BJ

0191 341 0031
www.o-de-v.co.uk

O de V is a quirky, confident, Fusion Steak House and Margarita Bar, exclusive to anyone who truly appreciates excellence and in which opulence takes centre stage. Since opening its doors in November 2010, Gary Cook, formally of Malmaison, has transformed this riverside eatery. Set on the banks of the Tyne, the restaurant has exceptional views of the city and pays homage to tradition whilst also celebrating the contemporary.

At O de V, you can expect to dine on the finest steaks, served entirely to your specification, fusing the finest ingredients from around the world with cutting edge flavours and technique.

Gary sources all produce locally, with meat coming from a local farm and abattoir, where his meat is personally stamped. Fish and seafood are sourced from the Fish Quay at North Shields and all the fruit and vegetables from the superb Grainger Market in the very heart of the city.

Here the team of award-winning chefs share more than just their culinary talents. Gary's other team members include his nephews Chris Cook, who is second in command and the newest addition to the team, Steven Cook.

The Cooks are passionate about bringing something fresh and unique to the North East with a restaurant that boasts a purpose-built, craftsman-made wine library, housing some of the world's most prestigious labels. The mezzanine Margarita lounge, with vaulted ceilings and luxurious decor is exclusive and modern with music provided by the resident DJ. Our outdoor seating area with patio heaters offers the perfect place to unwind with one of the specially blended Margarita cocktails, a glass of fine wine or perhaps a morning coffee, whilst enjoying the splendid views of the River Tyne.

The Cooks are passionate about bringing
something fresh and unique to the North East
with a restaurant that boasts a purpose-built,
crafts-made wine library housing some of the
world's most prestigious labels

RARE BREED PORK TERRINE

SERVES 12

🍷 *Las Manitos, Pinot Noir*
Argentina

Method

Place the pork shoulder in a pan with the goose fat and simmer for 2 hours 45 minutes on a low heat until the meat is soft and tender.

Cool down on a separate tray and shred into small pieces.

Line a terrine mould with Parma ham making sure the ham is overlapping.

Add seasoning and vinegar to the meat. Then spoon over 50ml of the goose fat and bind together. Place in the terrine mould. When the pork is set and sliced it will have a marbled look.

Fold over the ham then compress with a heavy object and place in the fridge for 24 hours.

To serve

Once set, slice the terrine into 12 portions. Serve on a plate, adding baby gherkins, crusty bread, drizzle of olive oil and rocket leaves to garnish.

Ingredients

2 kg pork shoulder
1 large tin (500g) goose fat
500g Parma ham
300g baby gherkins
300g rocket salad
12 slices crusty bread
salt and pepper
100ml sherry vinegar
drizzle of olive oil

ASIAN INFUSED FILLET STEAK

SERVES 1

Turi, Cabernet Sauvignon
Chile

Ingredients

1 medium sized fillet steak
1 onion (diced)
1 chilli
1 clove of garlic
tsp Tandori paste
50g rocket salad
25g courgette (thinly sliced)
25g yellow pepper (thinly sliced)
10g stem ginger (thinly sliced)
olive oil
seasoning to taste

Method

Infuse fillet steak with diced onion, fresh chilli, garlic and olive oil 24 hours in advance.

Stirfry courgette and pepper in a hot wok for 2 minutes.

Char-grill steak, sealing both sides for 4 minutes.

Leave resting for 2 minutes.

Prepare a plate to serve by garnishing with sliced stem ginger, stirfry vegetables and dressed rocket leaves.

Then flash grill the steak for 2 minutes each side.

To serve

Place steak on pre garnished plate on top of stir fried vegetables and serve immediately.

CHOCOLATE FONDANT

SERVES 12

*Pocas LBV Port
2003*

Ingredients

500g dark chocolate
500g unsalted butter
10 egg yolks
200g caster sugar
10 egg whites
150g self raising flour sieved
sprig of mint

Garnish

raspberries
1 tub of good vanilla ice cream
handful of hazelnuts (chopped)

Method

For the fondant

Begin by melting down the chocolate and butter together and leave to cool for 10 minutes. Place the yolks and 100g of caster sugar in a separate bowl and whisk together over boiling water until light and fluffy. Mix the remaining whites and the other 100g of caster sugar together to make a meringue mixture and then add this into the other egg mixture, folding in the flour. Finally add the melted chocolate to the mixture and beat together until completely combined.

Pour the mixture into the prepared moulds and cook for 10 minutes at 200°C or until the tops are slightly crusty and starting to come away from the mould. Remove from oven and leave to cool for at least 1 minute.

Very carefully, remove the fondants by easing them out of the moulds.

To serve

Tip fondant onto the middle of a plate. Garnish with 3 raspberries and a ball of ice-cream rolled in crushed hazelnuts. Serve immediately.

Chef's tip

It is usually best to start by preparing the moulds. Lightly brush the moulds with melted butter and then sprinkle the inside with sugar and set to one side.

170
THE PLATE RESTAURANT

Newcastle Marriott Hotel Gosforth Park, High Gosforth Park, Newcastle upon Tyne NE3 5HN

For reservations and further information please call 0191 236 4111 (select option 5)
www.theplaterestaurant.co.uk
www.newcastlemarriottgosforthpark.co.uk

There has been horseracing of one kind or another in the North East for the last 350 years. The first recorded Northumberland Plate was in 1833 and won by 'Tomboy'. Since 1882, the famous race has been held at High Gosforth Park. 'The Plate' is a play on words, referring to both the 'Northumberland Plate' awarded to the winner of the North-East's most prestigious annual horse race and the bespoke show plates on each setting.

As one of the North East's most famous sons (Robert Louis Stevenson) was quoted as saying: 'All speech is dead language until it finds a willing prepared hearer'. The tableside interaction between Chef de Rangs, Sommeliers, Sous Chefs and customers is one of the qualities that set 'The Plate' apart from the rest of the field. Menu descriptors are brief allowing servers to demonstrate their extensive menu knowledge. The service and style reflects a certain classic elegance and aims to use traditional values without being seen as old fashioned.

Several of the signature dishes including the Centenary Plate – Foie Gras Three Ways – Poached with Pickled Cherries, Seared with Warm Apple and Endive Salad and Foie Gras Crème Brulée with Ginger Tuille, draw their inspiration from the fact that Gosforth was originally called Goseford – literally the place where the Geese crossed the Ouse Burn.

The Plate Restaurant is located within the Newcastle Marriott Hotel Gosforth Park

HOME CURED SALMON, PINK GRAPEFRUIT AND CORIANDER

SERVES 4

🍷 *Kleine Zalze Barrel Fermented Chenin Blanc*
South Africa

Ingredients

200g salmon fillet
1 lemon (zest and juice)
1 orange (zest and juice)
1 pink grapefruit (zest and segments)
10ml white wine vinegar
60g sea salt
6 black peppercorns (crushed)
120g sugar
10g fresh dill
10g fresh tarragon
1 fennel bulb
100g mooli
2 radishes
20ml olive oil
1 packet micro coriander

Method

Place sea salt, peppercorns, sugar, zests of citrus fruits, finely chopped dill and tarragon into a bowl and mix thoroughly,. Add a little citrus juice to make a paste.

Place the salmon onto the kitchen foil then place the mixture on top and seal in foil. Refrigerate for 24 hours.

Remove the salmon from the fridge and wash off excess salt, pat dry with kitchen paper; and remove skin and brown flesh. Cut into approx 4 x 50g portions and refrigerate once more.

Peel mooli, then using a mandolin slice lengthways; blanch in boiling salted water for 1-2 minutes. Place in ice water and drain.

Remove root of fennel and slice very thinly on mandolin; place in iced water; repeat with radish.

Chop grapefruit segments into four, refrigerate; reduce the remaining citrus juices in a pan; once reduced, allow to cool; whisk vinegar and juice together, add olive oil, season to taste.

To serve

Pat dry the fennel and radish then place two slices of fennel on the right hand side of the plate. Add a little of the dressing to the mooli then place 4 – 5 strands of mooli on top of fennel. Scatter pink grapefruit over the mooli and then place radish slices on top.

Place salmon opposite the salad, place coriander on top of the salad, then drizzle dressing over both.

DOUBLE RIB-EYE OF LAMB, CONFIT OF SHOULDER & PORT THYME JUS

SERVES 4

Etchart Privado Malbec, Valle de Cafayete
Argentina

Ingredients

2 x 4-bone best end of lamb (French trimmed)
160g shoulder of lamb
100g duck confit fat
4 slices Parma ham
100g carrots(finely diced)
100g onion (finely diced)
100g celery (finely diced)

Vegetables
100g butter
8 baby carrots
8 baby leeks
8 baby turnips
40g skinned broad beans

Potatoes
2 large baking potatoes
1 onion, finely sliced
salt and pepper
100ml Port
200ml good lamb or veal glaze

Method

For the shoulder

Seal off lamb shoulder in roasting tray, pour over heated confit fat; cover with kitchen foil; place into the oven, 100/120°C for approx 1 hour or until tender; allow to cool, or until you can flake it down by hand.

Using some of the confit fat, sweat off the diced vegetables and add to the lamb confit.

Place 4 slices of Parma ham into double thickness clingfilm, place lamb confit on top and roll into a cylinder shape; refrigerate overnight.

For the potatoes

Cook baking potatoes in their skins until three-quarters cooked – allow to cool then remove the skin; cut into approximately 5mm thick slices, then, using a 30mm pastry cutter, cut out centre of potato; meanwhile, fry off sliced onion in confit fat until golden brown and keep warm.

Seal the lamb in a roasting tray and place in the oven (165-170°C for 10 to 15 minutes. The core temperature should reach 63°C).

Cook off vegetables separately in boiling salted water.

Reduce port to a sticky glaze; pour in lamb glaze and bring to the boil; cut shoulder into four equal portions and place in the oven to heat through.

Once lamb is cooked, remove from the pan and allow to rest; meanwhile, place the tray onto the stove and begin to finish off potatoes until golden brown (adding half of the butter for flavour).

To serve

Put three potato circles in the middle of the plate, adding the onions on top, then add three more potatoes and place the confit of lamb at the top right (approx. 1'o'clock on the plate). Reheat the vegetables in hot water then add to butter and season and place these just below the lamb confit.

DRAMBUIE PARFAIT, HEATHER HONEY CREAM AND POACHED RED FRUITS

SERVES 4

Late Harvest Sauvignon Blanc, Concha Y Toro Chile

Ingredients

Drambuie Parfait

1 egg yolk
1 egg
20g caster sugar
half leaf of gelatine
125ml double cream (semi whipped)
50ml Drambuie

Poached Red Fruits

40g raspberries
40g blueberries
40g blackberries (halved)
40g strawberries (quartered)
stock syrup
150g sugar
100ml water
half vanilla pod

Heather Honey Cream

60g Heather honey
100ml double cream (whipped)
100g raspberries (for sauce)

To Garnish

4 brandy snap discs

Method

For the parfait

Soak gelatine in cold water.

Place the egg yolk, egg, sugar and Drambuie into a heat-proof bowl.

Whisk over Bain-Marie until the ribbon stage (careful not to cook the eggs).

Add gelatine to warm mixture and whisk until gelatine dissolves; place into a clean bowl.

Allow to cool; fold in semi-whipped cream into egg mixture.

Pour mixture into Dariole moulds and place in the freezer.

For the poached red fruits and heather honey

Make stock syrup (add sugar, water and vanilla pod) place in a pan and slowly warm water until sugar dissolves; then bring to the boil.

Pour stock syrup over the berries and allow to cool.

Drain berries and reduce stock syrup; with the remaining raspberries, once reduced pass thorugh a sieve and allow to cool; whip the double cream, fold in the honey and place in the fridge.

Pass through a sieve and allow to cool.

To assemble

Paint a strip of coulis across the plate, place parfait onto strip, dress with berries on one side, coulis on the other.

To serve

Quenelle honey cream on top of parfait (chocolate garnish optional). Place brandy snap at bottom of parfait.

180
RIVERSIDE
RESTAURANT

Bridge End, Barnard Castle, Co Durham DL12 9BE

01833 637 576
www.riverside-restaurant.co.uk

The people of Barnard Castle have been keeping a delightful secret since 2007, but now, the secret is out; nestled on the banks of the river Tees, overlooked by the castle and the county bridge, is the Riverside Restaurant.

This hidden gem, founded on the principle of good food and service, is all about quality. Beginning with the freshest, finest ingredients available locally, and then crafted with skill and passion into food to die for, borne on the principles of good, honest, simple food, driven by the passion and creativity of chef Andrew Rowbotham and his committed team. Andrew says, "It takes more than a talented chef to create outstanding food and a lot of hard work and dedication goes into producing and sourcing fine ingredients. The Farmers, Fishermen, Growers and Artisan Producers are invaluable to make the Riverside what it is."

Inside the restaurant there is a real sense of warmth, enhanced by low beamed ceilings, an array of candles and Moorish scatter cushions.

Service is relaxed and efficient, with a friendly welcome and warm words to perfectly complement your dinner. The Riverside Restaurant is truly a destination that wears its heart on its sleeve.

With the success of The Riverside, Andrew and his family have taken on a major refurbishment of The Crown at Mickleton, Barnard Castle. A "Real Pub", along with everything that goes with it.

Inside the restaurant there is a real sense of warmth, enhanced by low beamed ceilings, an array of candles and Moorish scatter cushions. Service is relaxed and efficient, with a friendly welcome and warm words to perfectly compliment your dinner

SEARED FILLET OF CODLING, STEAMED SHELLFISH AND BROWN SHRIMP VELOUTE

SERVES 4

🍷 *Sauvignon Blanc, Kuki - Malborough - New Zealand*

Ingredients

1 codling fillet
4 live razor clams
200g live cockles
200g live mussels
100g fresh samphire
100g brown shrimps (peeled)
2 whole vine ripened tomatoes (skinned, de-seeded and diced)
butter
1 banana shallot (peeled, finely diced)
juice of ½ lemon
100ml white wine
100ml cream

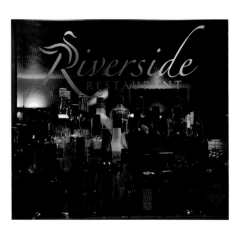

Method

For the steamed shellfish and brown shrimp veloute

Prepare the shellfish by cleaning the outside of the shells then submerge them in cold water (mix for 20 to 30 minutes prior to cooking to expel any sand or sediment).

Heat a pan with a tight-fitting lid over a high heat. When the pan is hot, add the razor clams, cockles, mussels, shallot and white wine and immediately cover the pan with a lid so that the clams steam.

Steam for 30 seconds to 1 minute, they should all open. Remove all of the shellfish onto a plate, strain the cooking liquid through a fine sieve into a clean pan then set aside.

When the razor clams are cool enough to handle, remove the clam flesh from the shells using your hands (reserve the shells). Discard any razor clams, cockles or mussels that have not opened fully during cooking. Remove the meat from the cockle and mussel shells (you can set aside a couple of each of the shells for presentation if you desire).

Chop the cooked razor clam meat quite thinly then set aside.

Return the reserved cooking liquid to the heat and bring to a simmer. Continue to simmer the mixture until the volume of liquid has reduced by half.

Add the cream, continue to simmer and whisk until the liquid has thickened slightly.

Add the sliced razor clams, lemon juice and butter to the mixture. Stir well until the butter has melted, add your chopped tomato, shellfish meat (chopped razor clam, mussels and cockles) and brown shrimps. Turn off the heat.

For the fillet of codling

Heat a frying pan until hot then season the codling skin with salt and pepper, add a little cooking oil to the frying pan and place the fillets in the pan skin side down. Cook for approximately one minute until skin begins to crisp, turn onto the flesh side and cook for a further minute. Turn off the heat.

To serve

Lay the opened razor clam shells in the centre of the plate and spoon the creamy mixture into the shell and around the plate. Lay the codling fillet across the centre and serve immediately.

FILLET OF DEXTER BEEF, SLOW ROASTED SHORT RIBS, MASH, PEAS, BROAD BEANS, REAL ALE JUS

SERVES 4

Chamuyo Estate
Argentina

Ingredients

Beef

4 x 4oz Dexter beef fillets
groundnut oil

Ribs

1 rack of (4 bone) Dexter beef short ribs (Jacobs Ladder Cut)

Real Ale Jus

1 large onion (peeled and diced)
1 carrot (peeled and diced)
2 sticks celery (peeled and diced)
½ leek (washed and diced)
2 cloves of garlic (peeled and crushed)
a couple of sprigs fresh thyme
500ml bottle of real ale

Method

For the ribs – Part 1 – The day before

Place the short ribs in a deep roasting tray, add half a bottle of ale and roast in pre-heated oven for 6 ½ hours at 160°C. Once cooked, turn off oven and leave for an hour before handling. Remove foil and cover a clean, flat baking tray in baking parchment then carefully lift the ribs and place fat side down on the parchment. Cover the ribs with parchment and cover with another flat tray. Weigh down with a couple of tins and refrigerate for a minimum of 4 hours. Pour all of the liquid stock from the tray into a bowl or jug and scrape the sediment from the tray. Refrigerate until later.

The following day

Take your fillet steaks out of the fridge to allow the core to reach room temperature.

For the real ale jus

Heat a saucepan, add a tablespoon of oil and sweat the onions, carrots, garlic and celery until soft then add the remaining ale and thyme and bring to the boil. Take the stock from the fridge, remove all of the hard fat from the top and discard, add the stock to the pan and simmer for 30 minutes. Then strain the liquid through a sieve. Return to a clean pan and bring to the boil, rapidly boil until the liquid has reduced by half in volume. Set aside until required. Reheat later.

For the ribs – Part 2

Pre-heat oven to 220°C. The ribs should be set up from the fridge and cut alongside the bones into 4 equal ribs. Trim and square all sides. Place the ribs skin side down uncovered in a non stick roasting tray for 15 minutes. Carefully turn over and roast skin side up for a further 15 minutes.

For the fillet steak

Heat a frying pan until very hot then coat the fillet steaks in groundnut oil and season with salt and pepper. Immediately sear in the pan. Turn over after 1 minute and continue to sear all of the outer edges 1 minute per side. Set the steak aside in a warm place and allow to rest for 3/4 minutes. This will cook medium rare, cook for longer depending on how you prefer your steak cooked.

To serve

Place the short rib onto the plate opposite the fillet and drizzle with Jus. Served best with mash, broad beans and peas.

Chef's tip

The key to sucess with the ribs is to ensure the tin foil is airtight and crimped around the lip of the roasting tray.

"MOODY BAKER" BREAD & BUTTER PUDDING, CHILLED LEMON POSSET, GINGER CRUNCH BISCUITS

SERVES 4

 Chateau Septy
Monbazillac

Ingredients

Chilled Lemon Posset

2 lemons (approx)
425ml double cream
125g caster sugar

Flavoured Butter

200g soft butter
large pinch nutmeg
large pinch cinnamon
zest of 1 orange

Puddings

4 x 150g mini bread loaves (Moody Baker -
Barnard Castle)
5 eggs
70g caster sugar
250ml of milk
300ml double cream
½ tsp vanilla extract
50g butter
dark brown soft sugar for topping

Ginger Biscuits

225g plain flour
2 tsp ground ginger
2 tsp baking powder
100g butter
100g caster sugar
½ tsp Bicarbonate of soda (dissolved in 1 tsp
hot water)
2 lge tbsp Golden Syrup (warmed)

Method

For the lemon posset

Zest the lemons then squeeze out and strain out 120ml juice.

Mix the cream, lemon zest and sugar in a non-stick pan. Bring to the boil, stirring occasionally until the sugar has dissolved, then simmer for three minutes. Take the pan off the heat and whisk in the lemon juice. Strain the mix into a jug, pressing the zest in the sieve to extract as much flavour as possible. Discard the zest.

Skim the froth off the top of the posset mix, then pour equal amounts into four shot glasses. Leave to cool. Cover the glasses with clingfilm and refrigerate for at least 4 hours.

For the bread and butter pudding

Cut the bread into 1cm slices, remove all crusts. Butter both sides of the bread using the flavoured butter. Arrange the bread to fit in your ramekin or small oven proof dish.

Separate the eggs – Keep all 5 yolks and 1 egg white. Whisk the egg yolks and white with sugar. Heat the milk and cream and vanilla until boiling. Pour over the eggs, whisking all the time. Pour the egg custard mixture over the bread and leave for 20 minutes.

Melt the remaining butter and brush the top of the bread then sprinkle with brown sugar.

Place dishes into a deep roasting tray, take the tray to the oven then fill the roasting tray with boiling water until the ramekins are almost half covered.

Take care not to spill hot water into puddings then gently push the roasting tray into the oven.

Bake at 200°C for approximately 20 mins until the custard has set.

For the ginger biscuits

Sift the flour, ginger and baking powder into a bowl. Rub in the butter. Add the sugar, then mix to a dough with the Bicarbonate of soda mixture and syrup. Roll the mixture out on greased baking sheets.

Bake in a preheated moderately hot oven 200°C for about 10 minutes. Once baked remove from the oven and cut with a 3.5cm round cutter.

To serve

Assemble as in the picture.

Chef's tip

The quantity of lemon juice is key to the success of the posset. The citric acid thickens the cream, and this makes it set when it's chilled in the fridge.

190
THE ROSE & CROWN

Romaldkirk, Barnard Castle, Co Durham DL12 9EB

01833 650 213
www.rose-and-crown.co.uk

The Rose and Crown at Romaldkirk is a charming 18th century coaching inn set on the middle green next to the old Saxon church known as the Cathedral of the Dale. Owned by Christopher and Alison Davy for the past 22 years, the R&C has gained an enviable reputation and has scooped some major national awards including Michelin Inn of the Year, Automobile Association Pub of the Year and Egon Ronay Pub of the Year. It is one of only three hotels in the North East with Automobile Association Red Stars as well as having been awarded two AA Rosettes for the past 16 years. The R&C features in all reputable and independent Food and Hotel Guides.

A daily changing four course dinner is served every evening in the oak panelled restaurant featuring the very best of seasonal and regional produce. In addition, lunches and suppers are served every day in the Bar and Brasserie, featuring a monthly changing menu. The Inn has twelve very comfortable en suite bedrooms of which two have private sitting rooms.

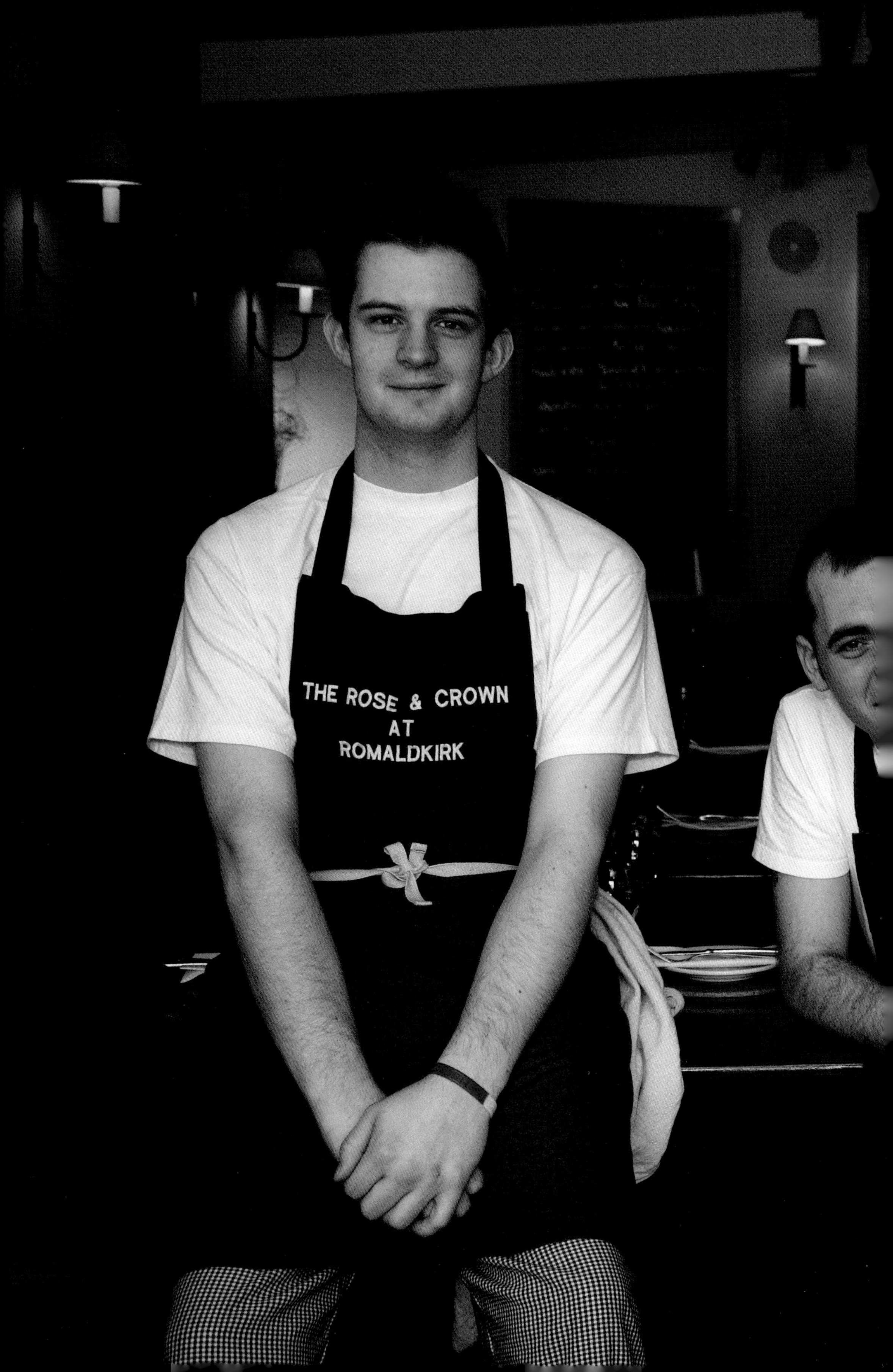
THE ROSE & CROWN
AT
ROMALDKIRK

The Rose & Crown is one of only three hotels in the North East with Automobile Association Red Stars as well as having been awarded two AA Rosettes for the past 16 years

SEARED MACKEREL, SEA SAMPHIRE, SAUCE VIERGE

SERVES 4

🍷 The Infamous Goose, Sauvignon Blanc, Wild Rock,
Marlborough 2009 New Zealand

Method

For the sauce and samphire

Sweat the shallot in a little olive oil until softened but without colour.

Remove from the heat and add the vinegar, olive oil and coriander seeds and leave to infuse.

When ready to serve, add the herbs and tomatoes and mix gently. Season.

Heat a frying pan with a little olive oil, add the samphire and toss over a medium heat for 5 minutes.

Remove from the heat and the pan and then keep warm.

For the mackerel

Place the frying pan back on the heat, add some more oil and fry the mackerel quickly on both sides until just cooked.

To serve

Place the sea samphire on plates.

Place the mackerel on top with the sauce around the fish.

Scatter sea salt on the fish and serve.

Ingredients

1 mackerel filleted and cut into 4 pieces
50g sea samphire

50ml olive oil
1 tbsp balsamic vinegar
1 tbsp lemon juice
5 coriander seeds (crushed)
1 shallot (finely chopped)
1 tomato, skinned, de-seeded (finely chopped)
1 tbsp fresh tarragon (chopped)
1 tbsp fresh coriander (chopped)
1 tbsp flat parsley (chopped)
1 tbsp chives (chopped)
Maldon sea salt

PINK ROASTED DUCK, CHESTNUT AND THYME RISOTTO, SEVILLE ORANGES

SERVES 4

🍷 *Chateau Haut Roc Blanquant, St Emilion Grand Cru, Dubois-Challon 2004, France*

Ingredients

2 fat duck breasts
200g risotto rice
1 onion (peeled and chopped)
1 leek (washed and thinly sliced)
1 knob butter
2 tbsp sunflower oil
500ml chicken stock
100g grated Parmesan cheese
50g preserved chestnuts (roughly chopped)
fresh thyme (chopped)

2 Seville oranges/ordinary oranges (halved with juice squeezed)
2 shallots (finely chopped)
125ml red wine
125ml Port
200ml chicken stock
2 tbsp redcurrant jelly

Method

To make the risotto

Melt the knob of butter and oil in a pan and sweat the onion and leek until cooked without colour.

Add the rice and stir well for 3 minutes.

Add a ladle of stock, stir well and cook until absorbed.

Keep adding stock in stages until the risotto is just soft to the bite.

Add the chopped chestnuts.

Stir in the Parmesan, add another knob of butter, some chopped thyme and then season.

For the sauce

Sweat the shallot off in a little sunflower oil until soft without colour.

Add the red wine and Port and reduce by half.

Add the orange juice and red currant jelly and reduce by half again.

Add the chicken stock and reduce again.

Season and reserve

Heat a frying pan. When hot, add the duck breast skin side down and seal for 4 minutes until coloured.

Transfer onto a baking sheet (skin side up) and cook in a hot oven (210°C) for 10 minutes.

Remove and season the skin side with salt and allow to relax for 15 mins in a warm place.

To serve

Re-heat the duck quickly in the oven. Slice onto the risotto and pour the sauce around. Serve immediately.

VANILLA PANNA COTTA, DARK TOFFEE CREAM

SERVES 4

🍷 *Nelson Estate, Noble Late Harvest, 2009, Paarl, South Africa*

Ingredients

Panna Cotta

300ml whipping cream
235ml full fat milk
1 vanilla pod
4 leaves gelatine
150g caster sugar

Toffee Cream

250g demerara sugar
250g salted butter
250ml whipping cream

Method

For the panna cotta

Soak gelatine leaves in cold water.

Put milk and cream into a pan and bring to a simmer.

Add sugar and dissolve.

Split the vanilla pod and scrape the seeds into the pan and remove from heat.

Squeeze excess water from the gelatine leaves and add to the cream and stir in until dissolved.

Pour the mixture into ramekin moulds, chill down in the fridge for 4 hours.

For the toffee cream

Melt the sugar in a pan slowly without burning.

Add butter and cream and stir until amalgamated.

Simmer for 10 minutes, strain, chill and reserve for use.

To serve

Turn out the panna cottas onto plates and serve with the dark toffee cream.

200
SEAHAM HALL

Lord Byron's Walk, Seaham, County Durham SR7 7AG

0191 516 1400
www.seaham-hall.co.uk

With numerous Michelin Stars and AA Rosettes over the past few years The White Room restaurant at Seaham Hall is the fine dining destination to visit in the North East.

The kitchen is headed up by new head chef Ian Swainson who joins the hotel from a number of Michelin Starred kitchens, with a reputation as one of the most talented young chefs in the industry.

His menu is heavily influenced by seasonality, with Swainson sourcing only the finest, freshest, locally sourced ingredients – indeed, the most succulent beef available is sourced from just down the road and the mackerel fished direct from the North sea waters.

The White Room restaurant is superbly designed and finished, making a special dining experience into something perfect. The hotel has 20 beautifully appointed bedrooms which give the guests of the restaurant the opportunity to stay over and enjoy Seaham Hall's extensive wine list.

When the superb cuisine is combined with 5 star service and one of the best spa's on the planet it is easy to see why Seaham Hall is the star of the North.

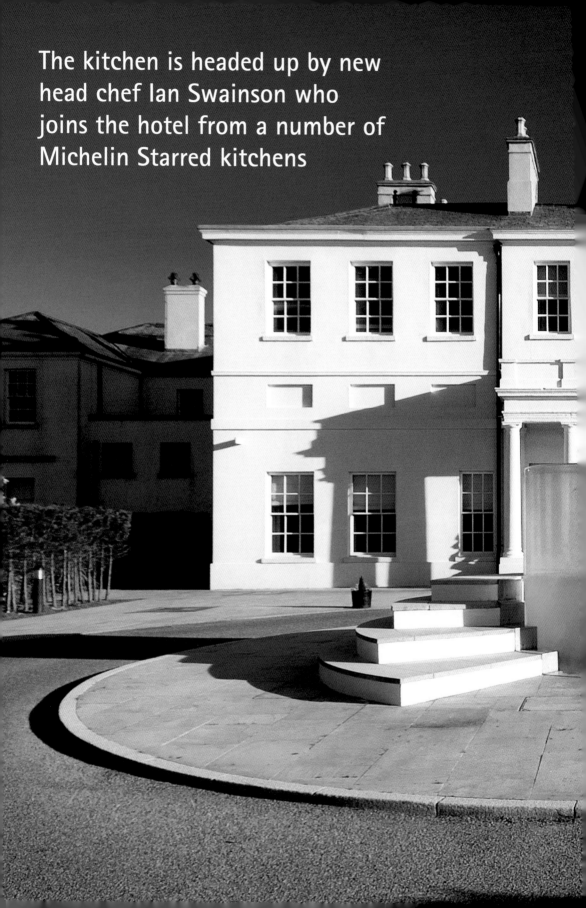

The kitchen is headed up by new head chef Ian Swainson who joins the hotel from a number of Michelin Starred kitchens

CHARRED MACKEREL WITH PICKLED RADISH, WASABI, MANGO AND AVOCADO

SERVES 4

🍷 *Wither Hills, Sauvignon Blanc, Marlborough, New Zealand, 2009*

Ingredients

2 x 160g mackerel fillet

Salsa

2 mangos
1 red long chilli
1 spring onion
coriander

Mango Purée

mango trim left from the salsa
20g sugar
20ml water

Avocado Purée

2 ripe Haas avocados
60ml olive oil
60ml water
60ml lime juice
8g salt

Pickled Radish

1 Mouli radish
100g sugar
100g white wine vinegar

Other ingredients

wasabi paste

Method

For the pickled radish

Take the mouli radish and peel it, then with a mandolin slice the mouli into thin slithers (so when you pick it up you can see your fingers through the slice). Mix the sugar and the vinegar and mix without any heat then put the mouli slices in, making sure that the radish is completely submerged. Leave to marinade for a minimum of 2 hours.

For the salsa

Peel and then carefully dice the mango, keeping all the waste (not the peel!) separate. Take the red chilli, cut it in half and de-seed it, then dice into small cubes. Add to the diced mango. The spring onion is then sliced at a long angle, as finely as you can, then add to the salsa mix. Finish by adding diced coriander, lime juice and salt. Mix together with a spoon and reserve in the fridge.

For the mango purée

Bring the water and the sugar to the boil to make a simple stock syrup, then cool down. Once cold, add to the mango trim and put everything into a food processor. Blend until smooth and pass.

For the avocado purée

Take the avocados and with a sharp knife cut in half around the stone, then open and remove the stone. Cut in half again and with a small knife and peel back the skin. Put the avocados and all the remaining ingredients into a food processor. Blend until smooth and pass.

To serve

Take the mackerel fillets and cut in half, then oil and cook under a grill at a high heat until the skin is charred. Then deglaze with lime juice and season with salt.

Take the wasabi, dilute it slightly with water and with the use of a paint brush, swipe some across the plate. Dress with radish then the mango salsa and finish with the hot mackerel and purées.

BEEF WITH PARSLEY PORRIDGE, OYSTERS AND SHALLOT MARMALADE

SERVES 4

🍷 *Brunello di Montalcino, 'Poggio Alle Mura' Cas tello Banfi, Tuscany, Italy, 2004*

Ingredients

500g beef strip loin
4 oysters

Tempura

100g plain flour
65g corn flour
20g baking powder
150ml sparkling water

Porridge

20g butter
5g garlic puréed
40g onion (finely dice)
100g porridge oats
600ml water

Parsley Purée

2 bunches flat leaf parsley
1 litre water

Shallot Marmalade

6 large shallots
50ml sherry vinegar
10g salt
10g sugar

Others Ingredients

30g parmesan
curly kale

Method

For the beef

Take the strip loin of beef and trim the outside so there is no fat or sinue left on, then cut in half lengthways. Cut in half again, this time the opposite way, so you end up with a square of meat. Reserve this for later.

For the parsley purée

Take the parsley and pick off the leaves. In the meantime, have a big pan of water rapidly boiling and throw in the parsley leaf to cook for 7 minutes (until the parsley breaks down in your fingers when rubbed). Then plunge into iced water. Reserve 50ml of the cooking liquor and cool down, then add both the liquor and the cooked, squeezed parsley to a food processor. Blend until smooth.

For the marmalade

Peel the shallots, then cut in half lengthways and slice into half moons as thinly as you can. Add this to a sauce pan with a little oil, the salt and the sugar. Cook slowly until all the liquid is gone and it is all caramelised. Add the sherry vinegar and cook down again until dry. Reserve and cool.

For the porridge

Take the onion, garlic and butter and slowly cook in a saucepan until soft, but not coloured. Add the oats and then the water, cooking slowly until the liquid has all been absorbed, then cook out.

To finish

Make the tempura flour: mix together, then slowly add cold water, whisking until made into paste. Open the oysters and flour, pat off and then put into the tempura paste. Deep fry in oil until golden and crispy at 170°C. In the meantime, have your beef colouring in a frying pan and then add to the oven, cook to the desired cuisson. Rest for a minimum of 5 minutes before serving.

Heat up the porridge, adding a little water to make pliable, then add teaspoons of parsley puree until a vibrant green colour has been achieved. Add grated parmesan and salt.

In the meantime boil some curly kale in salted water.

To serve

Put the porridge into a ring and press down, then place the curly kale on top. Add the beef, then the oyster and the shallot marmalade. Finish with a red wine beef sauce and serve.

CARAMEL SOUFFLÉ WITH NEWCASTLE BROWN AND BREAD ICE CREAM, SWEET WINE MARINATED GOLDEN RAISINS

SERVES 4

🍷 *Cockburns, Fine Ruby, N.V, Port*

Ingredients

Soufflé

50g sugar
108ml water
16ml whipping cream
70g sugar dissolved in a little water (10ml approx)
15g cornflour

Ice Cream

500ml Newcastle Brown
500ml milk
2 vanilla pods
200g egg yolk
150g sugar
100g granary dried breadcrumbs
100g sugar

Raisins

100ml Sauternes sweet wine
20g sugar
100g golden raisins

Other Ingredients

160g egg whites
40g sugar
4 ramekins

Method

For the soufflé

Bring the 50g of sugar to a direct caramel in a large saucepan, when the caramel is dark and bubbling add the water and cream, make sure that all the caramel is dissolved. Cool over ice, once cold mix with a whisk gradually into the corn flour to make a light solution.

In a separate pan bring the 70g of sugar to 121°C and pour into the corn flour solution and whisk in, to finish then add everything back onto the heat and whisk over a high heat until mixture has thickened up and the corn flour has cooked out, cool again.

With a brush and some soft butter line your ramekins, making sure that the whole inside is covered then line with sugar, cool.

For the ice cream

Take the milk, ale and vanilla and bring to the boil in a saucepan, in the meantime whisk the yolks and sugar until the mix looks light in colour. Once the liquid has boiled, add over the yolks and whisk to incorporate the two together, put back into a clean saucepan and on a low heat, stirring at all times bring to 84°C, pass, cool and put into a container.

For the sugar and breadcrumb mix (to add to the ice cream mix)

Caramelise the sugar and add the bread crumbs, mixing until properly incorporated and then pour the mixture out to cool on some greaseproof paper. Once the caramel is cold, add to a blender and blitz until a breadcrumb consistency is met, then add to the ice cream mix and freeze.

For the golden raisins

Bring the wine and sugar to the boil and add the raisins. Soak.

To finish and serve

Take 120g of your finished soufflé base and put into a round bottomed mixing bowl, in a separate bowl add 160g of egg whites and in a separate put have 40g sugar.

Start to whisk the whites and as they begin to foam add the sugar, carry on whisking until the mix becomes firm and silky, fold ⅓ of the mix into your caramel mixture, beat in, and then add the next two instalments of the whites ⅓ at a time, being gentler each time. Finally pour into the lined ramekin and cook in a pre heated oven at 165°C for approximately 8 minutes, until the mix has risen well and the soufflé looks golden.

Carefully place the soufflé onto a plate, scatter the raisins and ball the ice cream, this should be served immediately.

210
SECCO RISTORANTE

86 Pilgrim Street, Newcastle upon Tyne NE1 6SG

0191 2300 444
www.seccouk.com

In 2009 Hamed Fardoust became the owner of Secco, having previously managed the restaurant for 4 years.

Determined to build on Secco's award winning status, he continues to champion the very best in local, seasonal produce from the North East of England and the Southern tip of Italy.

The interior of Secco is designed to induce a sense of supreme well-being. It glows with rich colour, striking patterns and textured materials full of subtle detail.

Secco is a two storey venue which offers a haven of style and seriously good quality Italian drinking and dining, inspired by Salentino in Southern Italy.

On the First floor, Secco Blue Room serves cutting edge cocktails and drinks set in opulent surroundings. Featuring installations, paintings and filmwork by contemporary artists, it's a sophisticated place to relax and unwind with a great selection of cool tunes. Blue Room is a more intimate bar which can be hired for any private events or used to chill out in this more secret and elegant hide-away.

On the second floor, the restaurant specialises in a superb interpretation of authentic, yet simple Italian food "Alta Rustica", using the finest, seasonal ingredients from Northumberland and the best of Southern Italian staples which is complemented by a wine list befitting the finest Italian enoteca.

Secco Ristorante Salentino is listed in Restaurant Magazine's Top 100 Restaurants 2009, highest ranked Restaurant in the North East of England, winner of Best Newcastle Restaurant 2007 by the Gourmet Society and it was also Winner of a Harden's Remy 2006 when it was voted the "Best Italian outside of London".

On the second floor, the restaurant specialises in a superb interpretation of authentic, yet simple Italian food "Alta Rustica"

PANZAROTTI – OXTAIL RAVIOLI

SERVES 8

*Terre Al Sole,
Salento Primitivo*

Ingredients

1.5 kg of Oxtail
2 sticks of celery
1 onion
2 carrots
1 small chilli
2 cloves of garlic
50g of pancetta
1 tbsp of tomato purée
1 glass of red wine
50g of mascarpone cream
1 egg yolk
50g breadcrumbs
1 box of cherry tomatoes
bunch of fresh basil
Vincotto (dressing)

Pasta Sheets

6 cups unbleached all-purpose flour plus
additional for dusting (semolina flour)
5 large eggs, lightly beaten
2 tbsp salt
4 to 6 tbsp water
2 tbsp olive oil

Method

In a large heavy buttered pan sear the jointed oxtail until all surfaces are brown, remove to one side.

Finely dice the vegetables with garlic and fry with the pancetta, add basil, than deglaze with the red wine. Add tomato puree and fresh cherry tomatoes cover with water and simmer for approximately 3 to 5 hours until the meat falls from the bone.

Pass the cooking liqueur through a fine chinois, reduce in a pan and add vincotto.

For the dough

Mix all the ingredients to make the dough then knead it for 30 seconds. Transfer to a floured surface and let it stand, covered with an inverted bowl, for at least one hour to let the gluten relax and make rolling easier (best left overnight).

For the 3 pasta sheets

Divide dough into three equal pieces, then flatten each piece into a rough rectangle. Set the rollers of the pasta machine on its widest setting to begin with.

Lightly dust the first piece with flour and feed through rollers, gradually reducing the setting to narrow. Lay sheets of dough on lightly floured baking sheets to dry until leathery but still pliable, for about 15 minutes. Roll out the remaining pieces of dough in the same manner if required. (Covering with damp cloth).

For the stuffing

Mix the meat and a little bit of liqueur with the egg yolk, mascarpone and breadcrumbs to a fine consistency.

Pipe into the prepared pasta sheets.

To serve

Cook the ravioli and serve with the cooking liqueur. Garnish with a few drops of vincotto and basil leaves.

AGNELLO FARCITO – SHOULDER OF NORTHUMBERLAND LAMB

SERVES 4

Farnese,
Edizione Cinque Aoutoctoni

Ingredients

2.7 kg shoulder of lamb (boned and rolled)
small bunch of fresh mint
6 cloves of garlic
4 banana shallots
1 onion
4 carrots
6 sundried tomatoes
1 head of fennel (trimmed and quartered)
1 pint of vegetable stock
1 glass of red wine
zest of half a lemon

Method

Season the inside face of the lamb shoulder with salt and pepper.

Sauté the fine sliced shallots, sliced garlic, mint, fennel trimmings and shredded sun dried tomatoes in olive oil.

Spread the cooked mixture on the inside of the meat, sprinkle lemon zest over and roll and tie with butcher's string.

In a roasting dish, roast chopped onion, carrots and fennel trimmings. Deglaze with one glass of red wine, then sit the joint on top. Fill the tray up to half way with vegetable stock surrounded with quartered fennel.

Cover the joint in foil and place in a medium hot oven for 45 minutes.

Uncover the joint and allow to cook for a further 30 minutes.

Remove the joint and strain the sleek. Reduce to a sticky consistency.

To serve

Cut the lamb into 4 thick slices and serve with the braised fennel and sprigs of fresh mint.

TORTA ALLE PERE E POLENTA-PEAR AND POLENTA TART

SERVES 10

*Toscana,
Isole e Olena, Vin Santo*

Ingredients

220g butter
220g caster sugar
150g fine almond
200g flour
3 large eggs
1 tsp baking powder
5/6 pears
120g polenta
1 ready made sweet pastry base

Method

Begin by preheating the oven to 160°C.

Cook the pears in 50g of butter in a saucepan over a low heat for 10-12 minutes, or until the pears are soft.

Cream the remaining butter and sugar together in a bowl until pale and fluffy.

Stir in the almonds and beat in the eggs, one at a time, until well combined.

Beat in the polenta, salt, baking powder and vanilla extract until well combined. Finally, fold in the pears.

Spoon the mixture carefully into the readymade pastry base in a tin and bake for 55-60 minutes, or until golden-brown.

For the syrup

In a small saucepan, bring the remaining ⅓ cup of sugar, reserved pear slices, and ⅓ of cup water to a boil. Reduce heat to maintain a steady simmer and cook, undisturbed, until syrup thickens, about 10 minutes. Set aside.

While the tart cools, brush generously with the syrup.

To serve

Serve as in the picture with a fresh mint leaf.

220
SLALEY HALL

Hexham, Northumberland, NE47 OBX

01434 673 350
www.devere.co.uk

Nestled within 1,000 acres of Northumbrian countryside, you will find Slaley Hall, one of the De Vere Hotel's collection and home to Duke's Grill Restaurant. A unique hotel for a unique location, Slaley Hall has fabulous interiors and a team of passionate staff to make your visit extra special. A true foodie hotel that conjures up nightly feasts of local must-try dishes, the warmest of welcomes for centuries around awaits you at Slaley Hall.

The award winning Duke's Grill can be found in Slaley Hall's classic Edwardian drawing room. With low lighting, and intimate candle-lit tables, Duke's Grill captures an essence of Great British dining that is rarely seen in this day and age.

Making the most of Northumberland's harvest, from land, river and sea, Head Chef, Nick Clough, who has been at the helm of the team since summer 2010 has a simple philosophy when it comes to his dishes...legendary local ingredients, prepared to perfection.

Passionate about sourcing local produce, Clough supports local suppliers and believes that the tastiest dishes come from the freshest ingredients.

In Duke's Grill you will find classic British food with a contemporary twist and many dishes are prepared right at your table. The wine list is extensive and the drama and excitement are pure Slaley Hall.

Enjoy mouth-watering dishes, must-try legends and great stories to take home with you.

Duke's Grill is open from Tuesday to Saturday, 7pm – 10pm. Be sure to book in advance so as not to miss this Northumbrian gem!

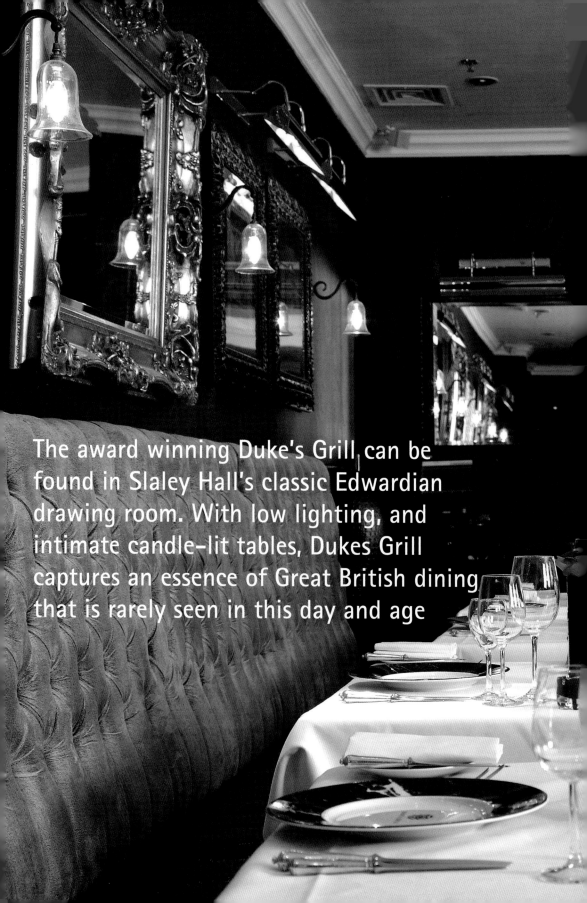

The award winning Duke's Grill can be found in Slaley Hall's classic Edwardian drawing room. With low lighting, and intimate candle-lit tables, Dukes Grill captures an essence of Great British dining that is rarely seen in this day and age

LOCALLY CAUGHT LOBSTER, WILD SALMON AND ASPARAGUS TERRINE, LOBSTER MAYO AND CITRUS PETIT SALAD

SERVES 6-8

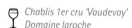
Chablis 1er cru 'Vaudevay'
Domaine laroche

Ingredients

Lobster terrine

2 large lobsters
½ celery
1 leek
1 onion
2 carrots
1 tbs tomato purée
100ml brandy
2 star anise
10 white peppercorns
4 bay leaves

Lobster Terrine

700g wild salmon (skinned and pin boned)
12 asparagus spears
500g high quality smoked salmon (long cut)
9 gelatine leaves

Lobster Mayo and Citrus Salad

2 eggs
Dijon mustard
cider vinegar
lobster oil
2 limes
Sakura cress

Method

For the lobster stock

Cook the lobster in boiling water for 6 minutes then remove and allow to chill. Remove meat from the lobster but keep the shell. Sweat off chopped celery, leek, onion, carrots and lobster shell and cook out until the vegetables are soft. Then add tomato purée and cook out for 2 more minutes. Add brandy and reduce until almost dry, then add star anise, peppercorns, bay leaves and cover with water. Cook out for 2-3 hours, remove from heat and pass through chinois.

Reduce this liquid down until you have 500ml and season.

For the lobster terrine

Bring salted water to a vigorous boil and add the asparagus. Cook for 1-2 minutes then remove and place into iced water for 1-2 minutes.

Cut salmon into 3 strips, equal in length, to the terrine mould (about 6 inches) then wrap tightly in clingfilm and poach in water for 2 minutes. Remove and chill.

Line the terrine mould with clingfilm.

Soak gelatine leaves in cold water until soft. Bring lobster stock to boil, squeeze excess liquid out of gelatine leaves and add to the lobster stock.

Line the terrine mould with the smoked salmon.

Pour a little of the lobster stock into the terrine then add meat from the lobster claws and press down firmly making sure the base of the terrine is covered.

Add some more stock then add a layer of the asparagus, again pressing down firmly making sure there are no gaps.

Keep doing this building up a layer at a time with more stock until terrine mould is filled.

Cover with clingfilm and place a piece of card cut to the exact size of the top of the terrine mould, wrapped in clingfilm, on the top. Weigh down and leave to set for 24 hours.

For the lobster mayo and citrus salad

Place 2 egg yolks in a mixer with 1 teaspoon of Dijon mustard and 1 teaspoon of cider vinegar. Mix and slowly add lobster oil until set to mayonnaise, season.

Peel and cut 2 limes into segments, mix with sakura cress and dress with lobster oil.

To serve

Assemble as in the picture.

224

RELISH NORTH EAST
SLALEY HALL

INGRAM VALLEY BLACK FACE LAMB RACK, MINT BUTTER CRUST, POMME ANNA, GIROLLE AND GREEN VEGETABLE FRICASEE

SERVES 4

🍷 *Spy Valley Pinot Noir, Marlborough*

Ingredients

Mint Butter

150g mint
50g parsley
1 banana shallot
6 garlic cloves
250g salted butter (softened)
1 lemon zest
½ lemon juice

Pomme Anna

2 large baking potatoes
200ml clarified butter

Fricasee

200g girolles, cleaned
50g fresh garden peas
50g mange tout
50g fine beans
75g butter

Lamb

2 best end rack of lamb – 7 bone, French trim

Method

For the mint butter

Blitz the parsley and mint in a mixer for 3-4 minutes.

Add shallots, garlic, lemon zest and lemon juice and mix again until smooth.

Add softened butter and mix until everything is bright green and smooth.

Spread butter between 2 sheets of parchment paper to 3-4 mm thick and refrigerate.

For the pomme anna

Peel potatoes and cut flat at both ends, then cut a with 5cm circular cutter.

Slice potato on a mandolin to 2mm thick so you have lots of thin circles of potato, and soak in water for 10 minutes.

Dry off the potato pieces and stack on top of each other, then pierce through the centre with a wooden skewer to hold in place.

Place the potato stack into a tall round mould, cover with clarified butter and cook for 15 minutes at 210°C until golden brown.

Pan fry the girolles in a little butter until lightly coloured.

In a pan of salted water, cook the green vegetables for 2 minutes, then transfer to the pan with the girolles and season.

For the lamb

Season the lamb and pan fry in butter until browned.

Cook in oven for 7-8 minutes then remove and allow to rest.

Place a piece of the mint butter over the lamb meat and grill lightly until butter is starting to melt.

To serve

Assemble as in the picture.

TROPICAL FRUIT AND SESAME "CANNELLONI", PASSION FRUIT AND MANGO SALSA

SERVES 6 -8

D'Arenburg, The Noble Chardonnay, Semillon, 2006, Mclaren Vale, South Australia

Ingredients

Mousse

2 egg yolks
60g sugar
40ml water
25ml pineapple juice
juice from 3 oranges
juice from ½ lemon
350ml double cream

Cannelloni

spring roll pastry
egg yolk
100g sugar
100ml water
sesame seeds

Salsa

1 mango
½ charentais melon
½ pinepapple
2 passion fruit
150g sugar
100ml water
1 orange
20g butter
sesame seeds

Method

For the mousse

Boil sugar and water to 120°C.

Whisk egg yolks and slowly pour in boiled sugar, whisking all the time.

Reduce orange juice and pineapple juice by half then add lemon juice and cool.

Whip the cream until stiff then fold this into the egg and sugar mix.

Slowly fold in the reduced fruit juices and refrigerate.

For the cannelloni

Cut a sheet of spring roll pastry to about 10cm by 10cm and wrap around a round pan handle, sticking it with egg to create. a tube.

Deep fry until golden brown then cool.

Make caramel with sugar and water, then brush the spring roll tube with caramel and sprinkle with sesame seeds.

When cool, pipe the mousse into the tube.

For the salsa

Finely dice the melon, mango and pineapple.

Take any trimmings and cook in the water and 100g of sugar until soft, then puree and chill.

Add the passion fruit to the puree and gently mix in the diced fruit.

Remove peel and pith from the orange and cut into segments, fry the orange with butter and 50g sugar and finish with sesame seeds.

To serve

Assemble in the picture.

230
THE SPICE CUBE

The Gate, Newgate Street, Newcastle upon Tyne NE1 5TG

0191 222 1181
www.thespicecube.com

Well-loved and well established, The Spice Cube is the only locally owned restaurant in The Gate development in the heart of Newcastle.
Passionate about real Indian food and inspired by the region's love of curry, owner Jalf Ali has set himself the personal challenge of introducing diners to a true taste of India.

Curry house cooking is out – along with one-pot sauces and westernised variations – and traditional dishes take centre stage. An experienced team led by head chef Ram Trivedi lovingly prepare each dish in the authentic way using technical know-how and drawing on first-hand knowledge of regional Indian menus.

Jalf's team of chefs recreate familiar favourite dishes in a way most customers have never tasted before – the real Indian way that is rarely attempted outside the homes of Indian families.

Then there are the 'Specials', the visionary fusions of flavours that are combined to create adventurous dishes of historical interest such as the popular Indian Railway Lamb Curry dish. In this book The Spice Cube shares its secret, award-winning Malabari Salmon recipe, which is not on the restaurant menu but helped it scoop the regional Curry Chef 2010 title.

It's not just the customers who think the Spice Cube's offering is rather special. Just recently, the restaurant was also awarded Best in North East at the national British Curry Awards, the Oscars of the UK's curry industry. A hard-fought and rather special accolade – and a great reason to try the restaurant out.

As director of The Spice Cube, Jalf Ali's ambition has always been to bring Newcastle in line with other UK cities such as London where Indian food is treated by chefs and diners with the respect and appreciation it deserves

CITRUS PRAWNS

SERVES 4

Pinot Gris A.C. Alsace
(France)

Method

Begin with preparing Part 1.

Wash prawns thoroughly and split in the middle.

Add the rest of the ingredients together from part 1 and gently marinate and leave for 20 minutes.

Then add all the ingredients together for Part 2 and leave to rest for 10 minutes.

Mix Part 1 and Part 2 together and leave to rest for 5 minutes.

Warm the grill on a medium heat for 5 minutes and then grill on a tray for 5-6 minutes.

To serve

Arrange as in the picture with a Mediterranean salad.

Ingredients

Part 1

12 tiger king prawns
50ml olive oil
3g salt
15g fresh ginger (finely chopped)
15g fresh garlic (finely chopped)
½ lemon juice

Part 2

4 kaffir lime leaf (chopped)
3 sticks lemon grass (chopped)
2 lemon (juiced)
15g brown sugar
8g paprika leaves
4g red chilli powder
salt to taste
8-10 curry leaves
50ml olive oil
2g toasted cumin powder
3g garam masala powder
10g Galangal

MALABARI SALMON

SERVES 2

*Cabernet d'Anjou Rosé A.C
(France)*

Ingredients

200g salmon fillet
600ml coconut milk
1 sliced red onion
4-6 sliced green chillies
2g mustard seeds
25g ginger juliennes
25g fresh garlic
½ tsp turmeric powder
½ lemon (juice)
salt to taste
8-10 curry leaves
50ml olive oil
2 tomatoes
2 chives
20g fresh tamarind pulp
50g potatoes
50g fresh baby spinach
2 pieces king prawn
1 sliced red pepper

Method

For the sauce

Heat oil in a pan, add mustard seeds and as they crackle add the curry leaf.

Add the sliced onion and ginger until they are translucent and then add the chillies and chopped tomatoes.

Add the turmeric, coconut milk, and tamarind pulp. Bring to the boil and then simmer for a further 3-4 minutes.

For the salmon

Coat the salmon fillets with olive oil, lemon juice and salt and then leave to rest for 10 minutes.

Add the salmon to the sauce and simmer for 1-2 minutes.

For the spinach and potato cake

Heat oil in a pan then add the peeled and crushed garlic mix for 2 minutes. Add fresh spinach and mix for a further 3-4 minutes.

Separately boil potatoes. Add to the garlic and spinach when ready. Mix for a further 8 minutes.

Grill the fish on a hot pan for 5 minutes taking care not to burn the spices.

To serve

Assemble as in the picture with the salmon resting on top of the spinach and the potato cake. Garnish with a king prawn and red pepper.

CARROT PUDDING

SERVES 4

🍷 *Orange Muscat & Flora Late Harvest Brown Brothers (Australia)*

Method

Peel and grate all the carrots.

Put the carrots and ghee in a pan and simmer until it is caramelised.

Pour the sugar and water into another pan and boil for 10 minutes to make the sugar syrup.

Grind the cardamom in a blender and add the powder form to the sugar syrup and mix thoroughly.

Add the pan of caramelised carrots to this.

Add the full cream dried milk (mawa) and mix thoroughly.

To serve

Serve on a plate and garnish the carrot pudding with sliced pieces of almond.

Finish with a scoop of vanilla ice cream and some fresh mint leaves.

Ingredients

500g fresh carrots
100g fresh cream dried milk (Mawa)
200g ghee
500g sugar
100ml water
10g green cardamom
5g almond (sliced)
1litre vanilla ice-cream
1 bunch mint leaves

240
WAREN HOUSE HOTEL

Bamburgh, Northumberland NE70 7EE

01668 214 581
www.warenhousehotel.co.uk

Two miles from the castle town of Bamburgh lies Waren House Hotel. This enchanting Georgian house, once owned by the third Lord Derwentwater, offers today's visitor a rare retreat for true relaxation, along with a central point for venturing through the delights of North Northumberland and the Scottish Borders. Known as "a perfect gem in the Secret Kingdom", the hotel is situated on the Northumbrian coast with stunning views of Holy Island and Budle Bay.

One highlight of the hotel is the beautiful and romantic AA-Rosette Gray's Restaurant where breakfast and dinner are served. Our team of four chefs, David, Graham and Mark, led by Head Chef Steve Owens, tempt diners to a gastronome's delight with a fusion of flavours derived from locally sourced ingredients obtained from suppliers within a forty mile radius. Herbs and other ingredients are grown in the hotel gardens. From the extensive cellar of vintage and fine wines, as well as several from the New World, a perfect complement to any meal can be found.

The hotel has fifteen guest bedrooms - decorated in a variety of individual styles. All are en-suite, some with walk-in showers and some with baths. Four of the bedrooms are accessed from the external courtyard and are on the ground floor.

The dedicated local staff have been complimented for their attentive, friendly and courteous approach to guests and visitors alike. So all in all, we believe the the Waren House Hotel offers our guests a friendly, relaxed, 'home from home' experience.

Known as "a perfect gem in the Secret Kingdom", the hotel is situated on the Northumbrian coast with stunning views of Holy Island and Budle Bay

LOCAL DODDINGTON CHEESE SOUFFLÉ, BEETROOT CHUTNEY, DODDINGTON CHEESE SAUCE

SERVES 4

🍷 *Sauvignon Blanc, Domaine des Sarret, d'Oc 2008*

Ingredients

Doddington Cheese Souffle

125g Doddington cheese (grated)
2 egg yolks
3 egg whites
40g butter
40g plain flour
1 tsp English mustard
100ml milk

Doddington Cheese Sauce

120ml whipping cream
250g grated Doddington cheese

Beetroot Chutney

1 tbsp olive oil
½ red onion (finely chopped)
1 garlic clove (finely chopped)
150g fresh peeled beetroot (chopped)
25g caster sugar
40ml sherry vinegar
1pt of water

Method

For the cheese souffle

Pre heat oven to 180°C.

Grease ramekins with unsalted butter and refrigerate.

Heat butter in a pan and add the flour and mustard (optional). Stir to a roux.

Stir in the milk and mix well to a gloss.

Fold in the cheese and allow to cool for 5 minutes.

Add egg yolks one at a time.

Whisk egg whites and then fold into the mix.

Fill ramekins ¾ full and cook in the oven for about 10 minutes until risen.

Remove from oven and serve quickly.

For the cheese sauce

Put cream and grated cheese in a glass bowl and melt together. Slowly over a low heat, pass through a sieve and season.

For the beetroot chutney

In a pan, add the olive oil, red onion, garlic.

Cook for 2-3 minutes, until just softened.

Add the beetroot, sugar, vinegar and water.

Simmer until reduced so hardly any liquid is left.

Season with salt and freshly ground black pepper and allow to cool

To serve

As in the photograph with dressed beetroot leaves and beetroot powder.

FILLET OF GLENDALE BEEF, OXTAIL RAVIOLI, ROAST ROOTS, PORT WINE AND SAGE JUS

SERVES 4

 *Rioja Crianza,*
Bodegas del Medievo

Ingredients

Fillet of beef

4 x 200g fillet steaks (tournedos)

Oxtail Ravioli (Mix)

400g oxtail
1 onion
1 carrot
½ leek
seasoning

Pasta

125g 00 pasta flour
pinch salt
1 medium sized egg
2 egg yolks

Roast Roots

1 stick of celery
12 small shallots
1 large carrot
1 large parsnip
½ a medium swede
sage butter

Sage Sauce

8 fresh sage leaves
50g unsalted butter
2 shallots (chopped)
100ml red wine
100ml port
400ml fresh beef stock

Method

For the fillet of beef

Pan fry fillets of beef to required degree in hot oil and finish with a knob of butter.

For the oxtail ravioli

Put oxtail with halved onion, whole carrot and leek into a casserole dish. Cover ingredients with water and cook for 3-4 hours at 150°C.

When cooked, remove from oven and take the meat from the bones. Dice with the vegetables and leave to one side in a bowl.

Reduce the remaining stock until sticky and add a splash of port, then add back to the meat/vegetable mixture.

To bind the oxtail mix, mould between your hands to form small balls and then leave to cool.

For the pasta

Blend all ingredients together and leave to rest.

Roll through a pasta machine set to the thinnest setting.

Cut out disks with a large round scone cutter.

Place a ball of oxtail mix on one disk and place another disk on top, then seal around edges with the help of cold water. Cook in simmering salted water for 3 to 5 minutes and remove.

For the roast roots

Cut root vegetables into required shapes, blanch in boiling water then refresh in cold water.

Brush with sage butter and lightly roast in the oven.

For the sage sauce

Sweat off chopped shallots in butter, add port red wine and sage then reduce until sticky and add beef stock. Reduce by half, whisk in a knob of unsalted butter and the correct seasoning. Then pass through a sieve.

To serve

As in the photograph garnished with fresh sage and potato pepper tuile.

RHUBARB MOUSSE, JELLY, SORBET AND COMPOTE WITH PRALINE CRUMBLE

SERVES 4

Muscat de Beaumes de Venise NV

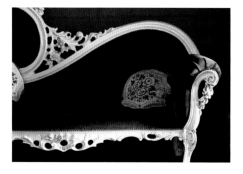

Ingredients

Rhubarb Mousse

250g rhubarb pulp
100ml whipped cream
200ml meringue (made using 2 egg whites and 50g sugar)
2 gelatine leaves
50ml Grenadine

Sorbet

100ml cold water
225g rhubarb (trimmed, chopped)
50ml grenadine
75ml glucose syrup
lemon juice

Jelly

200ml water
50ml grenadine
150g rhubarb (chopped)
2 leaves of gelatine

Praline Crumble

125g caster sugar
50g flaked almonds (toasted)
squeeze lemon juice
125ml water

Method

For the rhubarb mousse

Cook rhubarb and grenadine to a purée consistency and add the soaked gelatine while the mixture is still hot, then pass through a sieve. Leave to cool.

Whisk the cream to a ribbon consistency.

Make the meringue using the egg whites and sugar.

Fold all the ingredients together and pour into moulds to set as a mousse.

For the sorbet

Place rhubarb, glucose syrup, grenadine and water into a pan. Cover with a lid and simmer. Continue to cook until the rhubarb is tender then remove and cool.

Transfer the cooled rhubarb to a food processor and blend to a purée.

Pass the purée through a fine sieve.

Add lemon juice to taste.

Transfer the sieved rhubarb purée to an ice cream maker and churn until the sorbet is smooth and has set. Store in the freezer until needed.

For the jelly

Put water, grenadine and rhubarb in a pan and simmer for 5 minutes to infuse.

Strain liquid into a jug and retain rhubarb for compote.

Make up the liquid quantity to 200ml and reheat. Add soaked gelatine and pour into desired shaped moulds to set.

For the compote

Blend rhubarb from the jelly mix to use as a compote.

For the praline crumble

Heat water and sugar in a pan until amber colour, then add lemon juice.

Pour onto almonds in a metal tray and cool.

Blend the praline to a crumble before use.

To serve

As in the photograph, garnish with some rhubarb crisps.

250
RELISH NORTH EAST LARDER

AN INTRODUCTION FROM THE NORTH EAST'S MASTERCHEF FINALISTS

JOHN CARLTON
THE DUKE OF WELLINGTON

'The North East is incredibly fortunate to have the best natural larder on the planet. The sheer variation of produce is phenomenal. Our fields offer a happy breeding ground for cattle, dairy herds, pigs and lamb. Our unpolluted oceans and rivers are brimming with all types of fish. We've got gourmet game from wild rabbit, deer, pheasant and duck in many of our local farm shops. All this is offered to us on our doorstep! It's not only the chefs who make the North East a fantastic food destination; it's the local producers.'

DAVE COULSON
CASTLE EDEN INN

'Fresh Seasonal and Local are the main factors that I focus on while preparing my dishes. Each ingredient is delivered and prepared each day, whether it's Angela dropping off the free range eggs or Ken delivering the organic vegetables. The suppliers we choose are the best at producing what is most important to me from the surrounding area; meat, game, fish and vegetables. I find it highly rewarding foraging for ingredients close to home and my team of chefs all appreciate the level of care, skill and presentation that goes into each dish that leaves the kitchen.'

BAKERY

ALLENDALE
Allendale Bakery, Unit 2 Allen Mill, Allendale, Hexham,
Northumberland NE47 9EQ
01434 618 879
www.allendalebakery.com

*Allendale Bakery produces a wide range of quality crafted
baked goods, with a mind for local and organic ingredients.*

BORDER HOMEBAKE
Border Homebake, Hadrian Enterprise Park, Haltwhistle,
Northumberland NE49 9PJ
01434 321 684
www.traybakes.com

*Producers of high quality, traditional tray bakes such as
flapjacks, caramel shortcakes, brownies and many more.*

HEATHERSLAW BAKERY
Heatherslaw Bakery, Cornhill on Tweed,
Northumberland TD12 4TJ
01890 820 208
www.heatherslawbakery.co.uk

*Traditional methods and modern skill combine at the
Heatherslaw Bakery, where 150 year old water-driven
machinery mills the flour to be used in their own range of
cakes and biscuits.*

THE MOODY BAKER AT BARNARD CASTLE
22 Horsemarket, Barnard Castle, County Durham
DL12 8LZ
01833 638 844
www.themoodybakerco.uk

*An artisan bakery based in Barnard Castle, in the heart of
Teesdale. Since 2002 they have made it their mission to
create quality food from the finest ingredients and made
by hand. They pride ourselves on using locally sourced,
organic, or Fairtrade ingredients where ever possible.*

BEVERAGES

ALNWICK RUM CO
Aydon View, Alnwick, Northumberland NE66 1BF
01665 604 768
www.alnwickrum.com

*Alnwick Rum, the spirit of Northumberland was first
produced by the Alnwick Rum Co during the first world war.
A unique and complex blend of pot-still and continuous-
still runs from Jamaica and Guyana, you'll love its full, rich
taste and aroma combining dark chocolate with warm
spicy raisins and mature fruits.*

BIN 21
29 Newgate Street NE61 1AT
01670 504 901
www.bin21.com

*As well as over 300 different wines, bin21 offers something
unique to Northumberland-over 55 Malt Whisky's in stock
and access to over 2,000. A walk in bank vault full of fine
wines and Champagnes. The only commercial Humidor in
Northumberland, with an extensive range of fine cigars. A
range of local products including ales, lagers, Hand Crafted
Northumberland Gin, Lindisfarne Mead, local liqueurs and
spirits. 14 different ports including a range of Ruby, Tawny,
Crusted, Bottle Aged, Late Bottle Vintage and Vintage.
Exclusive parcels of fine wine and ports that they source
through specialist suppliers.. And so much more!*

BEVERAGES

CARRUTHERS AND KENT
3A Elmfield Road, Gosforth, Newcastle upon Tyne,
Tyne and Wear, NE3 4AY
0191 213 1818
www.carruthersandkent.com

*A new independent fine wine company in the North East
of England. It was born out of a passion for the fine things
in life; Wine, first and foremost, closely followed by food,
closely followed by their desire to share this passion for
wine and food with customers in the form of good old
fashioned service.*

*The fine things in life are not necessarily the rarest or the
most expensive, but to get on their shelves, those fine
things have to taste good, and be great value for money.*

HIGH HOUSE FARM BREWERY
Matfen, Newcastle upon Tyne NE20 0RG
(Visitors center) 01661 886192
(Sales) 01661 886769
www.highhousefarmbrewery.co.uk

*Founded in 2003, by fourth generation farmer Steve Urwin,
High House Farm is a traditional non-intensive farm
with a mixture of arable (wheat, oil seed rape and barley)
and livestock (sheep and cattle) that since 2001 has also
produced award-winning real ale.*

LINDISFARNE MEAD
St.Aidans Winery, Holy Island, Northumberland
TD15 2RX
01289 389 230
www.lindisfarne-mead.co.uk

*Lindisfarne Mead is a unique alcoholic fortified wine
manufactured on the Holy Island of Lindisfarne. The honey
which is used in the production, it is vatted with fermented
grape juice, herbs, and the pure natural water .*

MICHAEL JOBLING WINES LTD
PO Box 90, Ponteland, Newcastle Upon Tyne
NE20 0WZ
0191 378 4554
www.michaeljoblingwines.com

*A specialist in finding interesting wines from smaller
growers as well as sourcing good value wines from the
larger producers. All are wines that we would personally
choose to drink. Their focus is private customers as well as
quality restaurants within the North East.*

PUMPHREY'S COFFEE LTD
Bridge Street, Blaydon, Tyne and Wear NE21 4JH
0191 4144510
www.pumphreys-coffee.co.uk

*Freshly roasted coffee and locally blended teas are some of
the delicious products available from Pumphreys.*

COOKWARE

STANGERS COOKSHOP
101 St Georges Terrace, Jesmond, Newcastle upon Tyne
NE2 2DN
0191 281 8536
www.stangerscookshop.co.uk

Stangers Cookshop is based on St Georges Terrace in the heart of Jesmond, Newcastle upon Tyne. They pride themselves on product knowledge and strive to make your shopping experience a memberable one. Alongside popular retail brands you will find exclusive professional cookware.

DAIRY

ACORN DAIRY
Garhorne Farm, Archdeacon Newton, Darlington,
Co. Durham DL2 2YB
01325 466999
www.acorndairy.co.uk

Acorn Dairy was the first organic dairy in the country processing milk from its own cows and delivering directly to the customer. Acorn is a family concern, run by Gordon and Linda Tweddle and the next generation, Graham and Caroline.

THE CHEESE SHOP
The Cheese Shop, 6 Oldgate, Morpeth,
Northumberland, NE61 1LX
01670 504 434
www.thecheeseshopmorpeth.co.uk

The Cheese Shop is, as the name suggests, the place to go for cheeses of all kinds. Over 150 kinds of cheese are represented here, so try a few!

DODDINGTON DAIRY
North Doddington Farm, Doddington, Northumberland,
NE71 6AN
01668 283010
www.doddingtondairy.co.uk

Doddington Dairy is situated on a family farm, nestled at the bottom of the Cheviot Hills in the Glendale Valley of Northumberland. Cows graze contentedly here on the farm. They use the fresh whole milk from these cows to produce a range of traditional raw milk cheeses or to create a luxury ice cream for you to savour.

DURHAM COW CHEESE COMPANY
8 Ashbrooke Court, Hutton Henry, Hartlepoool,
Cleveland TS27 4QY
01429 836819/0782 453 5512
www.durham-cow-cheese-company.com

Soft cheeses made from cow's milk to the highest standards of quality and taste. Winner of the Blue Cheese Category in the Tesco Cheese Challenge, 2009.

MINCHELLA & CO
Minchella & Co. 11 Ocean Road, South Shields
NE33 2HT
0191 456 1905
www.minchella.co.uk

Minchella pride themselves on producing ice cream using the highest grade of quality ingredients, which has notably scored them a reputation second to none.

MORWICK DAIRY ICE CREAM
Morwick Farm, Acklington, Morpeth, Northumberland,
NE65 9DG
01665 711 210
www.royaldouble.com

Ice Cream from prize winning Ayrshire and Holstein cows in 18 different flavours. Stop by the ice cream parlour where they also serve coffee and cakes.

THE NORTHUMBERLAND CHEESE COMPANY LTD
Green Lane, Blagdon, Seaton Burn, Northumberland
NE13 6BZ
01670 789 798
www.northumberlandcheese.co.uk

For those who appreciate premium quality cheese, then Northumberland Cheese Company with its traditional methods of craftsmanship, which have stood the test of time, is a must.

FARMSHOPS

BLAGDON FARMSHOP
The Milkhope Centre, Blagdon, Newcastle Upon Tyne
NE13 6DA
01670 789 924
www.blagdonfarmshop.co.uk

*Blagdon only sell food that has been produced by farms
that are either organic or follow traditional farming
methods that are kind to the natural environment. Blagdon
Home Farm is one of only 24 LEAF (Linking Environment
and Farming) demonstration farms in the country. The
LEAF standard is your assurance that the goods have
been produced using methods that comply with high
environmental standards. Their philosophy is that what is
good for you is good for the countryside.*

BROCKBUSHES FARMSHOP
Brocksbushes Farm, Corbridge, Northumberland
NE43 7UB
01434 633100
www.brockbushes.co.uk

*Featuring pick-your-own strawberry and raspberry fields,
Brockbushes is perfect for those who really appreciate fresh
produce.*

COUNTRY HARVEST FARM FOODS
Unit 2, Hurworth Road,
Aycliffe Industrial Estate, Newton Aycliffe
DL5 6UD
01325 300 931
www.meats.co.uk

*Country Harvest was established in 1989 and has
successfully provided the finest hotels and restaurants with
the best quality of meats and poultry.*

HERDING HILL FARM
Herding Hill Farm, Shield Hill, Haltwhistle NE49 9NW
01434 320175
www.herdinghillfarm.co.uk

*Featuring rare breeds and other high quality farm produce.
Stop by with your new purchases at the lovely coffee shop
for a snack afterwards.*

FINE & SPECIALITY FOODS

JULIANS VEG
01434 632 948
www.juliansveg.co.uk orders@juliansveg.co.uk
*Julian supplies and delivers locally grown seasonal fruit and
vegetables, local free range eggs, freshly baked bread and
a wide variety of fresh fruits, salads and herbs from quality
North East suppliers. Currently, they deliver quality fresh
produce to homes, schools, holiday cottages, shops and
restaurants.*

THE CORBRIDGE LARDER
18 Hill Street, Corbridge, Northumberland, NE45 5AA
01434 632 948
www.corbridgelarder.co.uk

*They have a fantastic range of fine food in their online deli
where you can buy wine, beer, hampers, cheese, chutney,
jam, tea, coffee, cereals, oils and food gifts. In the modern
supermarket age, the Corbridge Larder Deli and Coffee shop
stands for good old fashioned value, the quality of their
food is the key to their success.*

MMM_NEWCASTLE
Unit 12-13, Grainger Arcade, Newcastle upon Tyne,
NE1 5QF
07801 357 314
www.mmm-food.co.uk

*With a philosophy to sell foods from close to home, they
sell a wide range of organic products. Their products range
from store cupboard basics to the more unusual and exotic,
such as garam masala and juniper berries.*

FISH

CRASTER KIPPERS
L Robson & Sons Ltd. Craster, Northumberland
NE66 3TR
01665 576 223
www.kipper.co.uk

*L. Robson & Sons Ltd. is a fourth generation family business
specialising in the traditional method of oak smoking
kippers and salmon. Situated in Craster, a small fishing
village on the Northumberland coast, the company still
cures the fish in the original smokehouses which are over
130 years old.*

LINDISFARNE OYSTERS
West House, Ross Farm, Belford, Northumberland
NE70 7EN
01668 213870
www.lindisfarneoysters.co.uk

*Pacific Oysters are available for sale all year round, having
been carefully reared in the North Sea using only the
natural resources in the seawater for their food. All oysters
are accompanied with their own health mark and dispatch
centre approval number to ensure quality*

TAYLOR SEAFOOD
3 Cliffords Fort, North Shields, Tyne and Wear
NE30 1JE
0191 2571 555
www.taylorseafood.co.uk

*Fantastic local fresh fish every day from North Shields Fish
Market. See the stunning displays and try both local and
exotic fish. A huge range of fresh and frozen produce with
seafood platters freshly made to order.*

MEAT

GREENBRAE
Newton Farm, Harbottle, Morpeth, Northumberland
NE65 7DP
01669 650 012
www.greenbrae.co.uk

Located in the heart of the Coquet Valley, Greenbrae produce beef, lamb and rare breed pork in all forms, where the animals are born on the farm and reared using age old techniques.

FREEMAN CATERING BUTCHERS
Unit 353, Dukesway, Team Valley Trading Estate,
Gateshead NE11 0PZ
0191 456 0297
www.freemancateringbutchers.co.uk

A family run business based in Gateshead, with over 50 years of experience and proud to be the National Catering Butcher of the year 2009.

HENRY HIRST (PROVISIONS) LTD
7 Wesley Drive, Benton Square Industrial
Estate, Benton, Newcastle upon Tyne NE12 9UP
0191 266 1515
www.henryhirst.com

Provide a wide range of top quality bacon products including sliced bacon, dry cure bacon and gammon joints.

KIELDER ORGANIC MEATS
Dunterley, Bellingham, Northumberland NE48 2JZ
01434 220 435
www.kielderorganicmeats.co.uk

Kielder Organic Meats supply a wonderful selection of free-range organic eggs and organic vegetables as well as delicious organic products, home-made on the farm by their butchers.

NORTHUMBERLAND POULTRY
Thistleyhaugh Farm, Longhorsley, Morpeth,
Northumberland NE65 8RG
01665 570 629
www.northumberlandpoultry.co.uk

Northumberland Free Range Poultry provides organic free-range chickens, ducks and guinea fowl to a wide range of local outlets.

WARREN BUTTERWORTH BUTCHERS
Unit 5, Westway Industrial Park, Ponteland Road,
Throckley, Newcastle upon Tyne NE15 9HW
0191 229 6060
www.warrenbutterworth.com

Warren Butterworth Catering Butchers has been supplying the catering sector for over 35 years. Only by supplying the finest meat, poultry and game have they earned their reputation as one of the leading Catering Butchers in the North East of England.

PARTNERSHIPS & FOOD ASSOCIATIONS

LOVE FOOD

91 Galgate, Barnard Castle DL12 8ES
www.lovefood.me

Love Food is delighted to be working with several restaurants featured in this book, including the Riverside Restaurant, Barnard Castle and The Morritt, Greta Bridge, in its aim to help promote and support local food producers and food-related businesses in the North Pennine Dales of North East England. Love Food is a wide partnership project managed by Teesdale Marketing and which is funded by the Big Lottery Local Food Scheme, North Pennine Dales LEADER Programme and Durham County Council.

PRESERVES, DRESSINGS & SAUCES

CHAIN BRIDGE HONEY FARM

Horncliffe, Berwick upon Tweed, Northumberland
TD15 2XT
01289 386 362
www.chainbridgehoney.co.uk

Chain Bridge Honey farm offers all varieties of high quality honey and honey based products, from honey mustard to beeswax candles.

HOT STUFF CHILLI COMPANY

3 Hastings Terrace, New Hartley,
Northumberland NE25 0SF
0191 237 3240
www.hotstuffchillicompany.co.uk

Hot Stuff Chilli Company is a family run Northumberland business making chilli sauces, Ketchups, jams and spice blends.

JEN'S JAMS

2 Bernard Terrace, Pelton Fell, Chester Le Street
DH2 2RD
0191 389 2707
www.jensjams.co.uk

Jen's Jams produce a range of preserves at home in Jen's kitchen. Production is limited to home-made quantities ensuring that every pan is given the time and attention to create delicious high quality sweet and savoury preserves.

RED RASCAL....TASTE ME LOVE ME

www.redrascal.co.uk
A rustic sweet chilli sauce and a sweet chilli ketchup. A sweet and savoury sumptuous blend with a gentle kick and an eruption of big red tastes bursting with flavour to excite the pallet! It's made with fresh red chillies and delicious ripe plum tomatoes and is an amazing accompaniment for most savoury foods for example eggs, meat, poultry and fish.

SMOKED FOODS

BYWELL FISH & GAME SMOKERY
Vallum Farm, Eastwallhouses, Newcastle upon Tyne
NE18 0LL
01434 672 770
www.bywellsmokery.co.uk

*At Bywell Smokery they appreciate the availability and
quality of the local fayre. They source the best quality raw
materials and know that if you only use the best they will
always have satisfied customers.*

SWALLOW FISH LTD
2 South Street, Seahouses, Northumberland NE68 7RB
01665 721052/720580
www.swallowfish.co.uk

*Cited as one of the possible places of the invention of the
modern Kipper, Swallow Fish has a long tradition of making
smoked fish in their on-site smokery, using the same
methods that have been used since their establishment in
1843. As well as smoked produce, Swallowfish also offer a
wide range of fresh, seasonal fish from the north sea and
provided by a close network of trusted suppliers.*

SWEET FOODS

BECKLEBERRY'S
Cowen Road, Blaydon on Tyne NE21 5TW
0191 414 1180
www.beckleberrys.co.uk

*Beckleberry's are manufacturers of Beckleberry's luxury
fresh ice creams and real fruit sorbets, as well as Artisan
handmade desserts.*

DAVENPORT'S CHOCOLATES
The Chocolate Studio, Unit 31, Evans Business Centre,
Orion Business Park, North Shields NE29 7SN
07813 954 368
www.davenportchocolates.co.uk

*Chocolates hand-made with passion and presented with
care. Each chocolate is artistically decorated by hand,
and beautifully presented in our stylish and elegant
contemporary packaging. They endeavour to create a
wonderful chocolate experience.*

CONSETT POPCORN COMPANY
Consett Popcorn Company, 32 Briarside, Consett, Co
Durham DH8 0AS
01207 582 691
www.consettpopcorn.webs.com

*A company that produces entirely natural, grown-up
popcorn with a twist. With flavours like hot chilli and
fennel, garlic and herbs and sweet cinnamon spice,
the Consett Popcorn Company offers something a little
different.*

NORTHUMBRIA FUDGERY
9 Eastcroft, Stanhope, Co Durham DL13 2NS
01388 529 428
www.northumbriafudgery.co.uk

*Specialising in an extensive range of handmade, luxury
fudges that will suit a wide variety of palates.*

PROOF OF THE PUDDING
Heckley High House, Alnwick, Northumberland
NE66 2LQ
01665 602 505
www.theproofofthethepudding.co.uk

*Homemade sticky toffee, chocolate and sticky ginger
puddings, dessert sauces, traditional steamed puddings
including marmalade with orange liqueur and the exclusive
Alnwick Rum Christmas pudding are just some of the fine
goods on sale here.*

THE CAKE ROOT COMPANY
Northfield Farm Cottage, Glanton, Alnwick,
Northumberland NE66 4AG
01665 578 842
www.thecakeroot.co.uk

*The Cake Root is the name that sisters Fiona Woodcock
and Jane Slater have given to their unique bakery
business. From their farmhouse kitchens in Glanton and
Longframlington they produce interesting cakes based on
root vegetables.*

YUMM! CUPCAKES
07900 180 932
www.yummcupcakes.com
*Bespoke cupcakes freshly baked to order, perfect for any
occasion and corporate event! Weddings, Christenings,
Birthdays etc.*

BARRASFORD ARMS

Hexham, Northumberland NE48 4AA
01434 681 237
www.barrasfordarms.co.uk

BATTLESTEADS

Wark on Tyne nr Hexham, Northumberland
NE48 3LS
01434 230 209
www.battlesteads.com

BLACKFRIARS RESTAURANT &
BANQUET HALL

Friars Street, Newcastle NE1 4XN
0191 261 5945
www.blackfriarsrestaurant.co.uk

BOUCHON BISTROT

4–6 Gilesgate, Hexham, Northumberland
NE46 3NJ
01434 609 943
www.bouchonbistrot.co.uk

THE BROAD CHARE

25 Broad Chare, Trinity Gardens, Newcastle upon
Tyne NE1 3DQ
0191 211 2144
www.thebroadchare.co.uk

CASTLE EDEN INN

Stockton Road, Castle Eden, Hartlepool, Cleveland
TS27 4SD
01429 835 137
www.castleedeninn.com

COLMANS

182 – 186 Ocean Road, South Shields,
Tyne & Wear NE33 2JQ
0191 456 1202
www.colmansfishandchips.com

DABBAWAL

69-75 High Bridge Street, Newcastle upon Tyne
NE1 6BX
www.dabbawal.com

THE DUKE OF WELLINGTON INN

Newton, Northumberland NE43 7UL
01661 844 446
www.thedukeofwellingtoninn.co.uk

FINBARR'S RESTAURANT

Waddington Street, Flass Vale, Durham City,
DH1 4BG
0191 370 9999
www.finbarrsrestaurant.co.uk

GREENHOUSE BRASSERIE

Quarryfield Road, Gateshead College, Gateshead
NE8 3BE
0191 490 2414
www.greenhousebrasserie.com

HEADLAM HALL

Headlam, Nr Gainford, Darlington DL2 3HA
01325 730 238
www.headlamhall.co.uk

HOTEL DU VIN & BISTRO

City Road, Newcastle Upon Tyne NE1 2BE
0191 229 2200
www.hotelduvin.com

MALMAISON NEWCASTLE

Quayside, Newcastle upon Tyne NE1 3DX
0191 245 5000
www.malmaison.com

THE MORRITT

Greta Bridge, Nr Barnard Castle, Co. Durham
DL12 9SE
01833 627 232
www.themorritt.co.uk

O DE V

Pipewellgate House, Pipewellgate, Gateshead
Quayside, Tyne & Wear NE8 2BJ
0191 341 0031
www.o-de-v.co.uk

THE PLATE RESTAURANT

Newcastle Marriott Hotel Gosforth Park, High
Gosforth Park, Newcastle upon Tyne NE3 5HN
0191 236 4111 (select option 5)
www.theplaterestaurant.co.uk

RIVERSIDE RESTAURANT

Bridge End, Barnard Castle, Co Durham DL12 9BE
01833 637 576
www.riverside-restaurant.co.uk

THE ROSE & CROWN

Romaldkirk, Barnard Castle, Co Durham DL12 9EB
01833 650 213
www.rose-and-crown.co.uk

SEAHAM HALL

Lord Byron's Walk, Seaham, County Durham
SR7 7AG
0191 516 1400
www.seaham-hall.co.uk

SECCO RISTORANTE

86 Pilgrim Street, Newcastle upon Tyne NE1 6SG
0191 2300 444
www.seccouk.com

SLALEY HALL

Hexham, Northumberland, NE47 OBX
01434 673 350
www.devere.co.uk

THE SPICE CUBE

The Gate, Newgate Street, Newcastle upon Tyne
NE1 5TG
0191 222 1181
www.thespicecube.com

WAREN HOUSE HOTEL

Bamburgh, Northumberland NE70 7EE
01668 214 581
www.warenhousehotel.co.uk

MORE QUALITY RECIPE BOOKS
AVAILABLE FROM THIS PUBLISHER

Relish North East – From the bustling city life in Newcastle, to the multitude of sleepy, rural villages, the North East has something for everyone. An introduction from the North East's best known chef, Terry Laybourne, kicks off this culinary adventure through a rich and diverse region, with many varied recipes for you to try at home, including a selection from the North East's two Masterchef finalists John Carlton and David Coulson plus many others from award wining chefs across the region.

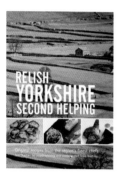

Relish Yorkshire – Second Helping – Featuring a foreword by celebrity chef Tessa Bramley, this second edition features all new recipes from Yorkshire's greatest chefs including Michelin Starred James McKenzie from The Pipe and Glass and Steve Smith from The Burlington plus Richard Allen from The Fourth Floor at Harvey Nichols and many, many more. A must have for any hearty food lover with Yorkshire pride.

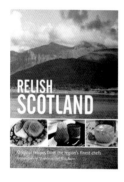

Relish Scotland – With over 300 Pages of Scotland's finest recipes, this book takes you on an epic journey from Edinburgh to Glasgow, across to Aberdeen and then up to the Highlands and Islands. An introduction from TV celebrity chef Nick Nairn prepares the palate for recipes from nationally acclaimed restaurateurs such as Tom Kitchin, Martin Wishart and Geoffrey Smeddle. With breathtaking pictures of the views and venues, Relish Scotland promises to make for very interesting reading for both foodies and tourists alike.

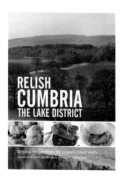

Relish Cumbria – Over 50 exclusive recipes from some of Cumbria's finest Country House Hotels and acclaimed restaurants including Nigel Mendham at The Samling, Russell Plowman at Gilpin Lodge Hotel and Andrew McGeorge at Rampsbeck Country House Hotel. Packed with innovative recipes and stunning photography to match the stunning landscape, Relish Cumbria makes a fantastic addition to your cook book library.

Relish Publications – is an independent publisher of exclusive regional recipe books featuring only the best and brightest critically acclaimed chefs and the venues at which they work, all showcased with superb photography. They also work with some chefs individually to produce bespoke publications tailored to their individual specifications. Since 2009, Relish has fostered a national presence, while maintaining friendly, personalised service that their highly professional team prides themselves on.

For more information about current and future Relish books, as well as information about the chefs and restaurants featured in them, visit www.relishpublications.co.uk

RELISH
PUBLICATIONS